ON EVERY PLAY

ELEVEN

MEN

BELIEVED

◇

The story of how the St. Louis Rams
rose from the cellar to the Super Bowl.

SP
SPORTS PUBLISHING INC.

www.ramsbooks.com

ST. LOUIS POST-DISPATCH
©2000

Editor: **Mike Smith**

Designer: **Tom Borgman**

Cover design: **CORE**

Photo editors: **Larry Coyne and Tom Borgman**

Chief copy editor: **Tom Klein**

Copy editor: **Mark Colosimo**

Research: **Gerald Brown, Stephan Thomas and John Duxbury**

Sports page designers: **Rob Schneider, Tricia Haugen and Chris Snider**

Coordinating editors: **Joseph J. Bannon Jr., Marie Ethen, Terry N. Hayden and Bob Rose**

Paperback: ISBN: 1-58261-258-7
Hardcover: 1-58261-296-x

Published by the St. Louis Post-Dispatch
and Sports Publishing Inc.

www.ramsbooks.com

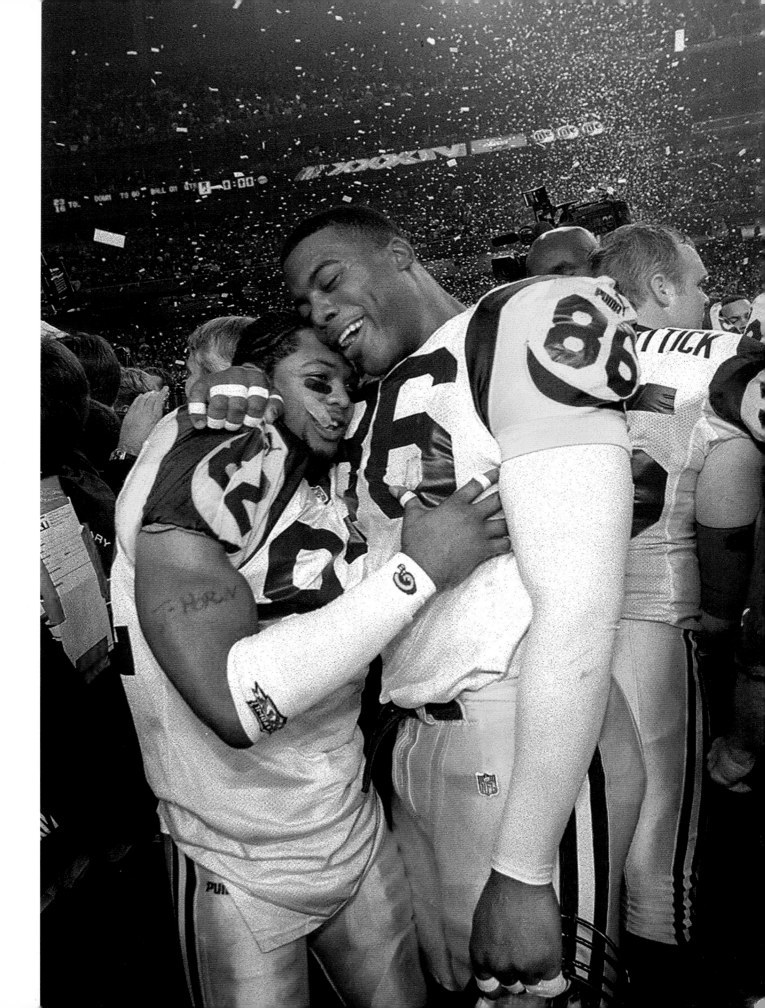

forewordforeword foreword forewordforewordf

By Bernie Miklasz

———————◇———————

The 29th of August was a bright, sunny Sunday for everyone but the Rams. Ominous clouds were forming above the grounds of Rams Park, threatening to cover another football season in darkness and hopelessness.

Coach Dick Vermeil, his eyes blinking faster than usual, met with the media to address a crisis: the team's devastating loss of starting quarterback Trent Green to a season-ending knee injury. The night before, in a preseason game against the San Diego Chargers, Green went down in a heap of torn ligaments and broken dreams.

After an encouraging, exciting preseason, this was a shocking blow. The Rams were mourning the cruel loss of their new leader. But the requiem would end as soon as the relentlessly upbeat Vermeil walked into the press room to deliver a bold message.

"We will rally around Kurt Warner," the choked-up but defiant Vermeil said. "And we will play good football."

And that was that.

Gotta believe. Gotta go to work.

Onward into the great unknown with the great unknown, Kurt Warner.

Kurt Who?

Warner had spent the 1998 season on the Rams' roster as a third-string quarterback, but we didn't know much about him. Now, it was time to inspect. An hour after Vermeil expressed his faith in him, Warner stood in a hallway outside the Rams' locker room, answering questions, his back pressed against the wall. It was the perfect pose, really, considering the team's desperate state. But Warner was cool, composed. No signs of stage fright.

"I've always felt that I was capable of leading a team in the NFL and being successful at this level," Warner said. "We're going to come together. The guys are going to pick it up and rally around me. I'm ready to go. I'm confident. I think we will be a good football team."

As it turned out, Warner was wrong.

The Rams did not become a good football team.

They became a great football team.

Warner took over the Rams, and the Rams took over the National Football League, bobbing and weaving to a 13-3 regular-season record and a first-place finish in the NFC West. The former Arena Football League quarterback turned NFL stadiums into his own private pinball machines. Warner flipped the ball around, piling up the points, setting off bells and whistles, triggering the flashing lights and generally causing so much commotion that the national media rushed to St. Louis to chronicle a phenomenon.

Warner praised the Lord and passed the football. He went to the air and flew the Rams into Atlanta for Super Bowl XXXIV. Along the way, he threw for 4,353 yards and 41 touchdowns and sealed all these sweet Sundays with postgame kisses to his wife, Brenda, who waited by the railing at her first-row seat at the Trans World Dome.

Warner made connections with his Warner Bros. receivers. He appeared at the Rev. Billy Graham's crusade. He lobbed footballs on David Letterman's late-night TV show. He had a breakfast cereal named in his honor. He won the NFL's Most Valuable Player Award. Oh yeah, and he saved the Rams.

Too good to be true?

"No, he's too good not to be true," Vermeil said.

Warner proved that a nice guy can finish first, even if it takes him awhile to get there. Even if he has to wait four years to become the starting quarterback at Northern Iowa. Even if he gets cut by the Green Bay Packers.

Even if he has to work the overnight shift at the Hy-Vee store in Cedar Falls,

Iowa, stocking shelves for $5.50 an hour. Even if he has to spend three seasons with the Iowa Barnstormers in the Arena league, absorbing rug burns. Even if he has to cancel a tryout with the Chicago Bears after getting bitten on the arm by a spider.

Even if he has to go far from home, to Europe, to earn a shot back in the USA. Even if he has to sit on the bench and wait for a turn that may never come. Even after the Rams leave him unprotected in the 1999 NFL expansion draft. Even if the opportunity comes when another quarterback gets chopped down in the third preseason game.

"The biggest thing was just work hard and continue to dream," Warner said. "Never letting go of the work ethic that I learned from my parents and my coaches when I was small. No matter how many people told me I couldn't do it, I wasn't going to let go of it.

"As long as I believed it myself, that was good enough for me."

Warner believed. So did his teammates. And when Warner finally got that opportunity, he became the quarterbacking equivalent of another famous Missourian -- President Harry S Truman, who went from relative obscurity to the White House.

Was this destiny? The nomadic Warner and the Rams were meant for each other. After all, the team also had gone on a long, strange trip. The Rams went from Los Angeles to St. Louis with a losing streak so long that it stretched between the two cities. Warner was looking for a chance. The Rams were looking for a miracle.

And along came the polite, poised young man with the Johnny Unitas brush cut, an accurate arm and the instinctive ability to read defenses. Warner and the Rams barnstormed through the NFL, leading a shell-shocked league in points and yards.

This was no accident. The Rams reconstructed themselves during one offseason. Vermeil, 9-23 in his first two seasons, reinvented the team's offense. He hired a new offensive coordinator, Mike Martz, who diagrammed dizzying plays for dazzling play-makers.

The Rams acquired sensational halfback Marshall Faulk from Indianapolis for the low, low price of two draft picks. Faulk set the NFL record for combined yards from scrimmage in a single season. He had more than 1,000 yards rushing, more than 1,000 receiving. Faulk was double trouble for the defense. He covered so much ground, there must have been two of him out there.

The Rams signed guard Adam Timmerman to anchor the right side of the offensive line. They drafted rookie Torry Holt, the lightning-bolt receiver. Orlando Pace got leaner and meaner and became a Pro Bowl offensive tackle. Wide receiver Isaac Bruce cured his hamstrings and went deep again.

The offense raced out to early leads. And the Ram-tough defense made it stand up. Defensive end Kevin Carter sacked the quarterback. Middle linebacker London Fletcher disposed of the running backs. Outside linebacker Mike Jones scooped up fumbles. Cornerback Todd Lyght picked off passes. The defense finished No. 6 in the NFL.

Tony Horne returned kickoffs and threatened to break the land-speed record. Az-Zahir Hakim fielded punts and made his way down the field like a butterfly. The Rams were a complete team. The offense, defense and special teams all were capable of controlling a game.

The Rams went from worst to first, from humiliation to domination. The Trans World Dome became the Transformation Dome, as the Rams gave St. Louis a home playoff game for the first time in the city's 33-year NFL history.

The 1999 Rams were all about change. And Vermeil showed how. He improved the sagging morale of his men by running a lighter training camp and shorter practices. He gave the players more free time. And, of course, Vermeil gave them hugs. Lots and lots of hugs.

The Rams were a happy family. They started out as teammates and became brothers. Everyone loves an underdog, and Warner and the Rams were the feel-good sports story of the year. No wonder Vermeil cried so often.

NEW FACES GIVE FANS
REASONS TO BELIEVE

◇

By Jim Thomas

Dick Vermeil knows that 1999 is a make-or-break season for himself and his coaching staff. He knows he has to win "X" amount of games to be back in 2000.

So, what is the "X" factor? An 8-8 record? A playoff berth? Or 7-9?

Neither owner Georgia Frontiere nor team president John Shaw has provided the magic number.

"I think it's more or less been communicated in different ways, not from Georgia but from John," Vermeil said. "I understand that. I understood that when I came here."

He also understood that he was walking into the NFL's losingest franchise in the 1990s, a team that had endured seven straight losing seasons when he arrived in 1997.

"It was a low-percentage chance when I came here," Vermeil said. "All I had to do was study the history. But what we're trying to do is prevent history from repeating itself, and I feel good about where we are."

The fact that his job is on the line in '99 won't change his approach to the season.

"Not at all," Vermeil said. "I've said all along that if I do not get to finish my tenure here, I'll leave them a lot better football team than I received when I got here.

"I was told about how many talented young players they had when I got here. A lot of those guys are gone. First-round picks. Second-round picks. They're not here. So, the evaluation

Marshall Faulk arrived at camp and left an impression on even the most casual observers. He was a sleek sports car standing out in a garage of diesels.

Trent Green learned his lessons on the sidelines of San Diego and as a starter in Washington. His career seemed ready to blossom at quarterback in his hometown.

process was hurting me more than anything."

Much of the Rams' personnel emphasis in the offseason was directed toward correcting past mistakes, particularly the draft class of '96. Marshall Faulk, in effect, replaced Lawrence Phillips at running back. Trent Green replaced Tony Banks at quarterback. Torry Holt replaced Eddie Kennison at wide receiver.

The Rams spent a lot of money — $26.7 million alone in signing-bonus money for their draft class and their five big free-agent or trade acquisitions: Faulk, Green, offensive guard Adam Timmerman, linebacker Todd Collins and safety Devin Bush.

"This year we were very successful in getting the people we wanted," Vermeil said.

The early — repeating, early — read on the Rams' 1999 draft class is that they've hit on more players than in any previous draft class since moving to St. Louis in 1995. "There's more good football players here," Vermeil said.

Except for an outbreak of sloppiness against Chicago, the Rams were a very good football team this preseason when their regulars were on the field.

"When Trent Green was (healthy), watching him grow and watching our offense on the field, there was no question in my mind that it was a playoff offense," Vermeil said. "Green's better than I thought he was."

But Green's season-ending knee injury in the Aug. 28 exhibition game against San Diego dampened expectations. Common sense says it will be harder to win with Kurt Warner at quarterback.

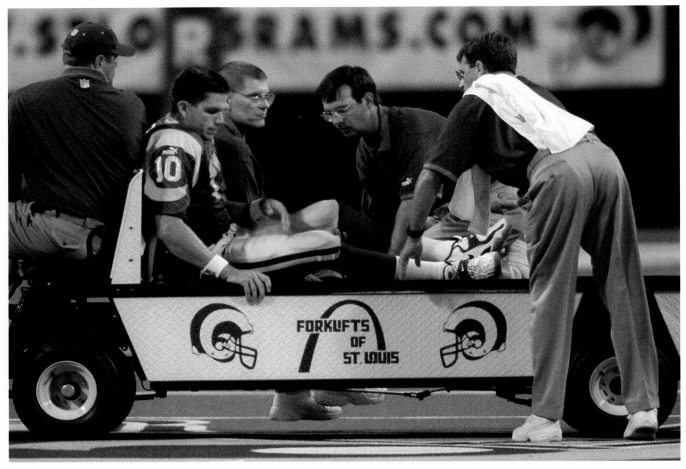

Trent Green was carted off the field after being injured in an exhibition game against San Diego. It was a sight that sickened Rams fans and demoralized a franchise. "This is the worst I've ever felt," team vice president Jay Zygmunt said.

"Yeah, I thought that," Vermeil said. "And I still feel that to a certain extent because Kurt Warner hasn't started 14 games like Trent played last year. ... But I feel good about him."

Vermeil said he has a gut feeling about Warner, a feeling reinforced by Warner's strong showing last week in the preseason finale against Detroit.

"Now, we just have to wait and see how it is in situations where it counts," Vermeil said. "When everybody's playing their 11 best players on every snap, and you're playing four quarters of football with your best people. As long as the quarterback can perform like an NFL starter, I think we have a chance to be a real good football team.

"... Kurt is going to play better than any of the No. 1 draft picks at quarterback this year."

Although this was the Year of the Quarterback in the NFL draft, Warner — formerly an Arena Football League and NFL Europe quarterback — doesn't mind the comparison and doesn't argue with it, either.

Dick Vermeil fought back tears the morning after losing his starting quarterback.

Kurt Warner was the man that Dick Vermeil turned to at quarterback. He had one exhibition game, against Detroit, to prove he was ready to take over. "I've got to go out and show teammates – show everybody – that I can run the team," he said.

Paul Justin (left) joined Kurt Warner in the Rams quarterback picture. But coach Dick Vermeil did not waffle in support of Warner. "Right now, he's our starting quarterback," Vermeil said.

"Going in, I would expect myself to play better, too," Warner said. "I don't expect there to be a dropoff from Trent to me. I'm going in with the expectation that I'm going to lead this team, and I'm going to be as successful as Trent would have been in the exact same situation."

The Rams have more playmakers on offense than they've ever had in St. Louis, so Bruce said Warner's assignment is obvious: "Just drive the car. Be the head, be the eyes, and we'll be the wheels."

Defensively, the Rams are undersized but very, very fast. The special teams ap-

Greg Hill (left) went to Detroit to fill the shoes of Barry Sanders, who had retired. He met up with former teammates, including rookie tackle Wille Jones, after the last exhibition game.

Marshall Faulk quickly gave young Rams fans someone to look up to. The Rams had an unknown at quarterback, an undersized defense and a receiver coming off an injury-shortened season. It was the perfect combination for a magical season.

pear to be stabilizing, what with Az-Zahir Hakim returning punts and the insertion of several front-line players on the coverage and return units.

"This is probably the most exciting team that I've played with, maybe since my freshman year of college," Faulk said.

Faulk thinks he can go where he wants to go in St. Louis. Namely, the playoffs year after year — and the Super Bowl.

"I believe we can," Faulk said. "I believe there's people here that deserve to get there. The D'Marco Farrs. The Kevin Carters. The Ike Bruces. It's a pleasure just to practice with him. I always thought I was a hard worker. I mean, Ike works

HARD."

As for Faulk, it's easy to see he has special skills. Despite a 13-day holdout at the start of training camp because of a contract dispute, Faulk already has displayed a smoothness to his running style and a gear or two that most running backs only wish they had.

"He's glaring," Vermeil said. "You don't have to be a talent scout to recognize his skills."

Vermeil said this team is more talented, will be more exciting to watch, and will win more games than his '98 and '97 Rams.

If not, Vermeil is fully aware of the consequences.

4 5 6 7 8 9 10 11 12 13 14 15 16

THE NEW QB PASSES MUSTER

———— ◇ ————

BY JIM THOMAS

There were a few bumps in the road, amid much congestion. But no car wreck. The Rams merely wanted Kurt Warner — in his first National Football League start — to "drive the car" in the Trans World Dome and let their gifted group of fleet-footed receivers do the rest.

Warner did just that, guiding the Rams to a season-opening 27-10 victory over the Baltimore Ravens. Warner threw two interceptions and lost a fumble. Once, he stumbled and fell while dropping back in the pocket.

But he also threw for 316 yards, the eighth-highest total for a Rams quarterback since the team moved to St. Louis in 1995, and he threw three touchdown passes.

The Rams just had too much on offense. Too many weapons. Too many options.

Double-cover Isaac Bruce, and Torry Holt was wide open. Put the clamps on Marshall Faulk in the running game? No problem. Faulk was a factor in the passing game with seven catches for 72 yards. Blanket Az-Zahir Hakim, and Ricky Proehl works his way open.

As Bruce said, "If you come in with a lot of bullets in your gun, they can't cover everybody."

The Ravens couldn't. Try as they might to rattle Warner and throttle Faulk, they couldn't keep the lid on the St. Louis passing game.

Warner toiled three seasons in the Arena Football League for the Iowa Barnstormers before making the Rams' roster last season as their third QB. At times against the Ravens, he made it look ridiculously easy. In the second quarter, Warner completed 12 of 15 passes for two TDs.

"We've always believed in Kurt . . . because we practiced against him all last year," defensive tackle Ray Agnew said. "It was just amazing the type of balls he threw. We (thought), 'Wow, this guy's pretty good.' "

Todd Lyght's interception in the second quarter helped to set up the Rams' first touchdown of the season. With a bye facing the Rams in Week 2, Lyght put the game in perspective. "We had to win. A loss would have been crushing," he said.

Isaac Bruce shook off two seasons of injury and frustration by catching eight passes in the opener. "I wanted to get back in the groove," Bruce said. "I'm fine now. I definitely will have a big season."

Scott Mitchell was sacked five times and felt the heat from the Rams defensive front all day. D'Marco Farr (left) and Ray Agnew ended this first-half drive. Agnew played the game with an injured hamstring.

KEY TO THE GAME

With the Rams up 17-10 early in the fourth quarter, QB Kurt Warner fumbled as he was sacked to give the Ravens the ball on the Rams 30. But the defense held as the Ravens lost 6 yards on the next three plays and missed a 54-yard field-goal attempt.

Torry Holt made his first NFL game memorable with three receptions, including a 20-yarder for a fourth-quarter touchdown.

	1ST	2ND	3RD	4TH	TOTAL
RAVENS	0	3	7	0	10
RAMS	3	14	0	10	27

SCORING SUMMARY

QTR	TEAM	PLAY	TIME
1st	**RAMS**	FG Wilkins 36 yds. 8:56	
2nd	**RAMS**	TD Williams 6 yd. pass from Warner (Wilkins kick) ..13:28	
2nd	**RAVENS**	FG Stover 25 yds. 6:00	
2nd	**RAMS**	TD Bruce 2 yd. pass from Warner (Wilkins kick) .... :33	
3rd	**RAVENS**	TD Stokley 28 yd. pass from Mitchell (Stover kick)..... :15	
4th	**RAMS**	FG Wilkins 51 yds. 8:56	
4th	**RAMS**	TD Holt 20 yd. pass from Warner (Wilkins kick)........2:40	

Kevin Carter had two sacks and forced a fumble. D'Marco Farr added another sack.

OFFENSE

RAVENS

PASSING	ATT	COMP	YDS	INT	TD
Scott Mitchell	40	17	188	2	1

RECEIVING	CATCHES	YDS	TD
Justin Armour	4	76	
Qadry Ismail	4	46	
Chuck Evans	4	27	
Priest Holmes	2	3	
Brandon Stokley	1	28	1
Greg DeLong	1	5	
Aaron Pierce	1	3	

RUSHING	RUSHES	YDS	TD
Priest Holmes	12	52	
Chuck Evans	3	8	

RAMS

PASSING	ATT	COMP	YDS	INT	TD
Kurt Warner	44	28	309	2	3

RECEIVING	CATCHES	YDS	TD
Isaac Bruce	8	92	1
Marshall Faulk	7	72	
Az-Zahir Hakim	5	63	
Torry Holt	3	36	1
Ricky Proehl	2	24	
Roland Williams	2	17	1
Chad Lewis	1	12	

RUSHING	RUSHES	YDS	TD
Marshall Faulk	19	54	
Justin Watson	1	5	
Robert Holcombe	4	1	
Kurt Warner	1	−1	

The one thing I've always admired about Warner is that he's a battler.
This is a guy who handles adversity very well. And he makes plays.

Charley Armey, Rams vice president of player personnel

Trent Green expected to start the season at quarterback. About the closest he got to the action was to walk the sidelines during pregame stretching.

Kurt Warner had two interceptions and a fumble, but he passed for 309 yards and three touchdowns. "Hey, he ain't going to the Pro Bowl right now," coach Dick Vermeil said after the game, "but we can win with Kurt."

GAME

1 SEPT. 12, 1999
TRANS WORLD DOME
RAMS 27
RAVENS 10

4567891011121314151 6

FINAL TAKE

By Bernie Miklasz

Nervous Rams fans can exhale. Kurt Whatever passed for 309 yards and three touchdowns to riddle the Baltimore Ravens in his first NFL start. He turned the NFL season-opener into his personal Arena Football League game and made a bunch of NFL scouts go back and check their reports to see how they missed this guy.

Kurt Whatever was good to go, grooving passes to Isaac Bruce, Torry Holt, Az-Zahir Hakim, Marshall Faulk, Ricky Proehl, Roland Williams and Chad Lewis. He would have hit Tom Fears and Elroy "Crazylegs" Hirsch had they been able to attend Sunday's induction into the St. Louis Ring of Fame at the Trans World Dome.

Kurt Whatever, a former Iowa Barnstormer, went barnstorming through Baltimore's defense. The Rams put so many fast receivers on the runway at the TWA Dome, the Ravens could only pick a blur and try to cover it. Opponents will need to study radar to get a read on the Rams receivers.

Kurt Whatever made a few errors but generally played so dashingly well that he made coach Dick Vermeil cry, made Rams owner Georgia Frontiere cry and made his wife, Brenda, cry when he rushed to the railing after the game to hand her a game ball. The victory belonged to him, and Kurt sealed it with a kiss to Brenda.

The Rams won 27-10 in front of 62,100 relieved fans. It's probably time to send e-mails to ESPN, CNN, Sports Illustrated, The Sporting News and all of the networks. Please inform various insiders, experts, telestrators, handicappers, Doctor Z's and talking heads that the Rams do have a quarterback.

And he has a name.

Tony Banks (left) hooked up with his former backup, Kurt Warner, after the game. Warner received a game ball from his teammates.

BOB & WEAVE DANCES ITS WAY ONSTAGE

———— ◇ ————

BY JIM THOMAS

The knockdown punches were swift and decisive. And once the Rams got Atlanta down, they didn't let up.

By the time a startling 35-7 Rams victory was complete, the Dirty Birds were road kill — 0-3 carcasses on the floor of the Trans World Dome.

"We're hungry," Rams cornerback Todd Lyght said. "We're hungry dogs. And we don't want to just eat the meat off the bone; we want to eat the bone, too."

The defending NFC champions were picked clean. The Rams did everything but grab Falcons QB Chris Chandler by the hamstrings and make a wish.

The Rams scored four touchdowns on their first four possessions. Midway through the second quarter, the Falcons were staring down the barrel of a 28-0 shotgun. After each blow was struck, and as the points piled up, the Rams did the Bob & Weave.

That's right. Atlanta has its Dirty Bird TD celebration. The Rams now have the Bob & Weave, compliments of rookie wide receiver Torry Holt.

Holt did the B&W after scoring the Rams' second touchdown.

"It's just a little bob and weave, you know, down low," Holt said. "I watched a little Muhammad Ali film, and I said, 'Let me see if I can take something from that.' And there are also a couple of rappers who do that type of thing."

The delirious crowd loved it. And for a week at least, the Rams are the toast of the town and the talk of the league.

"It's like a dream come true," defensive tackle D'Marco Farr said. "We've been here for five years now, and it's been a tough road. We've been trying to get to this point for a long time where everything's clicking.

"It almost brings tears to your eyes. We've worked so hard, and finally we have something going. We have the ball rolling."

Marshall Faulk emerged as a force in the Rams offense. He had 172 yards rushing and receiving and had a 47-yard run called back. "I could play like this every week when we get the ball movement that we did," he said.

Dexter McCleon clamped down on Chris Calloway to prevent a third-quarter catch with the Rams already ahead 35-7.

KEY TO THE GAME

The Rams staged their most impressive drive of the season in the first quarter. They took the opening kickoff and marched 80 yards on 17 plays and held the ball for 10 minutes 13 seconds. Robert Holcombe capped the drive with a 1-yard touchdown run.

Kurt Warner was spectacular in his second game. In the second quarter, his first three passes were for touchdowns. "We were just rolling, scoring every time we touched the ball," he said. His quarterback rating of 108.6 had the rest of the league taking notice. He was named NFC offensive player of the week.

D'Marco Farr earned the congratulations of Grant Wistrom (left) and Mike Jones after a tackle behind the line of scrimmage. After four losing seasons in St. Louis, Farr, an undrafted free agent, was moved by a 2-0 start. "It almost brings tears to your eyes," he said.

	1ST	2ND	3RD	4TH	TOTAL
FALCONS	0	0	7	0	7
RAMS	7	21	7	0	35

SCORING SUMMARY

QTR	TEAM	PLAY	TIME
1st	**RAMS**	TD Holcombe 1 yd. run (Wilkins kick)	4:47
2nd	**RAMS**	TD Holt 38 yd. pass from Warner (Wilkins kick)	14:53
2nd	**RAMS**	TD Bruce 46 yd. pass from Warner (Wilkins kick)	14:24
2nd	**RAMS**	TD Faulk 17 yd. pass from Warner (Wilkins kick)	6:35
3rd	**FALCONS**	TD Kozlowski 1 yd. pass from Graziani (Andersen kick)	7:32
3rd	**RAMS**	TD Warner 5 yd. run (Wilkins kick)	1:54

Chris Chandler left the game with a hamstring injury in the second quarter. After going to the Super Bowl the season before, Atlanta found itself 0-3.

OFFENSE

FALCONS

PASSING	ATT	COMP	YDS	INT	TD
Tony Graziani	22	14	152	0	1
Chris Chandler	9	5	28	1	0

RECEIVING	CATCHES	YDS	TD
Bob Christian	5	37	
Terance Mathis	4	51	
O.J. Santiago	4	29	
Byron Hanspard	2	40	
Chris Calloway	2	21	
Brian Kozlowski	2	2	1

RUSHING	RUSHES	YDS	TD
Byron Hanspard	17	50	
Tony Graziani	1	9	
Ken Oxendine	2	6	
Bob Christian	1	3	
Chris Chandler	1	0	

RAMS

PASSING	ATT	COMP	YDS	INT	TD
Kurt Warner	25	17	275	0	3

RECEIVING	CATCHES	YDS	TD
Marshall Faulk	5	67	1
Isaac Bruce	3	68	1
Torry Holt	2	47	1
Robert Holcombe	2	42	
Roland Williams	2	31	
Az-Zahir Hakim	2	17	
Jeff Robinson	1	3	

RUSHING	RUSHES	YDS	TD
Marshall Faulk	17	105	
Robert Holcombe	8	24	1
Justin Watson	6	20	
Isaac Bruce	1	11	
Kurt Warner	2	7	1

"I'm proud to be a Ram right now.
As proud as I've ever been.

Isaac Bruce

Isaac Bruce blew past 1998 Pro Bowl cornerback Ray Buchanan for a 46-yard TD, putting the Rams up 21-0. "It was just man-to-man, me against him, and I got behind him," Bruce said.

FINAL TAKE

BY BERNIE MIKLASZ

After the Rams offense had turned Atlanta's defense to grits with 35 points and 442 yards, the appreciative squad gave a game ball to offensive coordinator Mike Martz. We're surprised that Kurt Warner, Marshall Faulk, Isaac Bruce or Torry Holt didn't grab it and score another touchdown.

Martz's impact on the Rams is similar to that of Don Coryell on the football Cardinals about 25 years ago. Their coaching roots are connected. Martz learned offense from Ernie Zampese, who was Coryell's air-traffic controller in San Diego. Martz was raised on the Coryell playbook.

It is fascinating and thrilling, watching this partial duplication of history. The Rams play in the aptly named Trans World Dome. This offense is soaring. Top gun. Top fun. It's the most entertaining football played in St. Louis since Coryell and the Cardinals ascended to the playoffs in 1974 and '75.

"I've never had as much fun in my whole life," Martz said. "I probably will never have a group like this again. I'm under a star right now."

The Rams went over, under, through and around the Falcons in a 35-7 victory. Warner passed for 275 yards and three touchdowns. Seven receivers — the ever-increasing cast of Warner Bros. — caught passes.

And Martz sat upstairs in the coaching booth with a gleam in his eye, tormenting the Falcons. He was a mad football scientist, designing plays, making calls.

Martz gives all the credit to his talented players. He has so many choices, so many options, that calling plays for this team is like calling in a pizza order. Domino's doesn't offer as many combinations.

It's too early to make any firm conclusions about the Rams of '99. But it's certainly a nice vision, seeing a new version of Air Coryell glide through the Dome and touch down in the end zone.

Kurt Warner's postgame towel-wave was an early punctuation mark on a rags-to-riches saga.

PLAYING FOR A HIGHER PURPOSE

◇

BY JEFF GORDON

Kurt Warner never doubted himself. Brenda Warner never doubted her husband.

Still, it was a bit surreal watching him strafe the Atlanta Falcons on Sept. 26. The crowd at the Trans World Dome was up for grabs. Long-suffering Rams fans reveled in a 35-7 victory. So did Brenda.

She met Kurt when he was a student at Northern Iowa, where he finally started at quarterback as a fifth-year senior. He lost his first two games in that 1993 season, suffering a separated shoulder in the second defeat.

Brenda saw Kurt return to Cedar Falls, Iowa, after getting cut by the Green Bay Packers in 1994. He worked nights at a local grocery, freeing himself to work out on campus and to angle for NFL tryouts.

But the league didn't call again for three years. The Canadian Football League took a pass, too. So, he went to the Arena Football League, in which he narrowly missed getting cut by the Iowa Barnstormers after a rocky preseason debut.

She saw him put off a Chicago Bears tryout in the fall of 1997 so they could get married. On their honeymoon in Jamaica, a varmint bit him on his throwing elbow and caused it to swell. The Bears gave up on him.

Two months later, Brenda saw Kurt return from St. Louis dejected, certain that he had bombed his Rams tryout. But there he was after the Falcons game, having made playing quarterback in the NFL look so simple.

"It was unbelievable," Brenda said. "We had been praying to supernatural powers, and that came about supernaturally. It was so unbelievable. But if you have the strong Christian faith we have, anything is possible."

The Warners stand as testimony to that. Their son Zachary, 10, has made tremendous strides since suffering a severe head injury as an infant. Brenda has remained strong despite that accident and the tragic deaths of her parents in a tornado.

Winning is a minor concern compared with overcoming such real-life travails.

Still, the Falcons game was pretty cool.

"To see a man's dream come true is pretty exciting," Brenda said. "A lot of people have dreams and never get to reach them. To see it happen to somebody who is so worthy, with his character ... that's so fun to see."

After the win over Atlanta, the Warners returned to their West County home for some quiet family time. There was no night-clubbing for the Warners, no big-timing, only time with Zachary and their two younger children. "Big-timing?" Kurt said, laughing. "I don't know what that is."

The Warners went to the park, ate pizza and talked. Bath time brought the inevitable family water fight.

Then, Warner, the newest St. Louis sports hero, helped Zachary brush his teeth and find his pajamas.

"Whenever my head might get a little big, he lets me know," Kurt said. " 'You're here wrestling with me, helping me with this and helping me with that,' he's telling me. 'You're just Dad.' "

Warner smiles. Of all the compliments he has received, that's the most gratifying.

OCT. 3, 1999
CINERGY FIELD, CINCINNATI

RAMS 38
BENGALS 10

FOUR-TD SPREE MEANS A DAY OF OOHS & AZ

◇

BY JIM THOMAS

The Rams Express might derail, perhaps when it runs into the San Francisco 49ers.

But right now, this is not a football team — it's a runaway freight train.

After a 38-10 whipping of the inept Cincinnati Bengals, the Rams (3-0) are unbeaten, unchallenged and unbelievable. They have outscored their three opponents 100-27.

"Isn't that incredible?" safety Keith Lyle said.

Incredible. Amazing. Outstanding. Remember, these are the Rams we're talking about.

"Our offense is playing great, but we really haven't beat anybody of stature yet," wide receiver Isaac Bruce said.

Granted, in Baltimore, Atlanta and Cincinnati, the Rams have beaten squads with a combined record of 2-10. But the Rams routinely lost to such teams in the not-so-distant past.

"The Wizard of Az," wide receiver/punt returner Az-Zahir Hakim, put up a four-spot on the Bengals, with three touchdown receptions and an 84-yard TD on a punt return.

Bruce didn't score, but he had 152 receiving yards in about 2 1/2 quarters of work.

Meanwhile, it seems that Kurt Warner still thinks he's playing in the Arena Football League. He's the first player in at least 50 years — that's as far back as such records are kept — to throw three TD passes in each of his first three NFL starts.

It's just not supposed to be that easy in the NFL, in which almost every other game is decided by a touchdown or less. Maybe one or two times per season. But not three weeks in a row.

As the Rams walked off the field, several hundred Rams fans leaned over the stands shouting encouragement. One held a sign: "3-0. Now beat Frisco." Bruce pumped his fist in acknowledgment.

Cincinnati fans had good reason to hit the sack after the Rams put the Bengals to sleep. With the loss, the Bengals edged out the Rams as the first NFL team to lose 100 games in the '90s, but the franchises clearly were headed in opposite directions.

Az-Zahir Hakim (81) took time to catch a replay of one of his four touchdowns as Isaac Bruce (left) and Robert Holcombe also enjoyed the moment. Bruce had 152 yards in receptions, but said: "Hakim is the man. He can score from wherever. He's a great player."

	1ST	2ND	3RD	4TH	TOTAL
RAMS	7	14	14	3	38
BENGALS	3	0	0	7	10

SCORING SUMMARY

QTR	TEAM	PLAY	TIME
1st	BENGALS	FG Pelfrey 36 yds.	8:05
1st	RAMS	TD Hakim 9 yd. pass from Warner (Wilkins kick)	5:35
2nd	RAMS	TD Holcombe 1 yd. run (Wilkins kick)	11:38
2nd	RAMS	TD Hakim 51 yd. pass from Warner (Wilkins kick)	3:05
3rd	RAMS	TD Hakim 84 yd. punt return (Wilkins kick)	12:59
3rd	RAMS	TD Hakim 18 yd. pass from Warner (Wilkins kick)	2:32
4th	RAMS	FG Wilkins 19 yds.	10:42
4th	BENGALS	TD A. Smith 1 yd. run (Pelfrey kick)	2:26

Az-Zahir Hakim gained the marquee role in the latest Warner Bros. production, upstaging his fellow receivers with a four-TD day that included an electrifying 84-yard punt return for a touchdown. He was named NFC special teams player of the week.

OFFENSE

BENGALS

PASSING	ATT	COMP	YDS	INT	TD
Jeff Blake	23	12	114	0	0
Akili Smith	18	7	77	1	0

RECEIVING	CATCHES	YDS	TD
Darnay Scott	6	61	
Damon Griffin	3	34	
Marco Battaglia	3	30	
Carl Pickens	2	30	
Tony McGee	1	15	
Willie Jackson	1	13	
Michael Basnight	1	6	
Clif Groce	1	2	
Corey Dillon	1	0	

RUSHING	RUSHES	YDS	TD
Corey Dillon	15	39	
Michael Basnight	6	27	
Jeff Blake	2	14	
Akili Smith	3	12	1

RAMS

PASSING	ATT	COMP	YDS	INT	TD
Kurt Warner	21	17	310	0	3
Paul Justin	1	1	27	0	0

RECEIVING	CATCHES	YDS	TD
Isaac Bruce	6	152	
Torry Holt	4	58	
Az-Zahir Hakim	3	78	3
Marshall Faulk	3	17	
Ricky Proehl	1	27	
Robert Holcombe	1	5	

RUSHING	RUSHES	YDS	TD
Marshall Faulk	11	23	
Robert Holcombe	7	20	1
Torry Holt	1	14	
Justin Watson	6	13	
James Hodgins	2	3	
Kurt Warner	1	0	

KEY TO THE GAME

Az-Zahir Hakim sparked the Rams offense with four touchdowns. His third one, an 84-yard punt return in the third quarter, was the stuff of high-light film material. He muffed the punt then picked up the ball on a bounce and sprinted around and through the Cincinnati defense.

The thing is, we've got so many guys that are so special.
Each week, you see a different guy coming to the forefront and making plays.
This week it happened to be Az.

Kurt Warner

Isaac Bruce was stopped by Rodney Heath for a 12-yard gain in the first quarter. He burned the Bengals with five catches for 131 yards in the half.

GAME **3**

OCT. 3, 1999
CINERGY FIELD, CINCINNATI

RAMS 38
BENGALS 10

12345678910111213141516

FINAL TAKE

BY BERNIE MIKLASZ

OK, it's time to tell the tall tale to the rest of the nation.

One day, a mysterious figure named Kurt Warner stepped out of a tall Iowa cornfield and appeared in the Rams huddle to provide instant offense, instant mythology. He'd be the lead character in a football version of "Field of Dreams."

In three NFL starts, Warner has completed 68.8 percent of his passes for 894 yards and nine touchdowns. His quarterback rating is a ridiculous 125.0. He's accurate on short passes, long passes, touch passes, bullet passes, passes thrown to the side, passes feathered down the middle and passes made at his wife, Brenda, who always gets the first postgame hug.

At Cinergy Field, what we saw from Warner were three quarters of near perfection: 17 of 21 passing, a mere 81 percent, for 310 yards and three TDs. Coach Dick Vermeil rested Warner in the fourth quarter.

The blitzing Bengals came at Warner hard and tried to knock him out of this daydream-believer state of mind. Warner picked himself up and picked the Bengals apart. He handled the blitz, he found the holes in Cincinnati's coverage and he made the usual connections with the Warner Bros.

The first week, when he shook off some jitters and led the Rams to a win over Baltimore, Warner was a cute little story. After the second game, when he stuck darts into the Atlanta defense, Warner was a novelty. Now that he has done it three times in a row, he's at least a national curiosity.

"People can take me seriously or not take me seriously," Warner said. "It doesn't matter. We're going to attack people the same way. I thought I was someone to be taken seriously from Day One. But you know now they're going to have to take us all seriously."

Marshall Faulk (28) was one of the few who managed to catch Az-Zahir Hakim on his four-TD day.

DING-DONG, THE WITCH IS DEAD!

◇

BY JIM THOMAS

The report was filed shortly after 3 p.m. to the Missing Persons Bureau. By now, the search party will be out in full force ... looking for the Same Old Rams.

You know, those gridiron sad sacks who lost over and over again to the San Francisco 49ers. Seventeen straight times before this rousing 42-20 Rams victory.

Where are the Same Old Rams?

"They're long gone," said cornerback Todd Lyght, who had been 0 for 16 against San Francisco.

Where are the Same Old Rams?

"I don't even want to hear that phrase," said defensive end Kevin Carter, who had been 0 for eight. "Because after a while, the Same Old Rams are going to be the ones in the playoffs."

One last time: Where are the Same Old Rams?

"It's kind of a flip of the circumstances," said wide receiver Isaac Bruce, who had been 0 for eight. "Because we'd always be losing and get upset and want to fight. And that's kind of what the 49ers did."

In this upside-down, topsy-turvy NFL season, the Rams finally turned the 49ers on their heads. This time, they hit them with the early knockout punch, jumping to a 21-3 lead after one quarter.

"We've just got a squad right now," safety Keith Lyle said. "There were so many people ready to say: 'I told you so. The Rams aren't going to win.' But we're not about that this year."

What they're about is Kurt Warner, the Warner Bros. receiving corps, an underrated defense and markedly improved special teams. Warner continued his amazing run, completing 20 of 23 passes for 323 yards and five touchdowns.

"You know what he told me walking off the field?" Dick Vermeil said. "He said, 'You haven't seen the best of me yet, Coach.' "

Isaac Bruce, the first of his four touchdown receptions in hand, looked toward heaven as the Rams finally brought the 49ers to earth. Bruce was named the NFC offensive player of the week.

Jeff Garcia bore the brunt of another Rams charge, this time by Grant Wistrom. The Rams didn't manage any sacks, but the 49ers quarterback was under siege most of the day and threw three interceptions.

Ben Wittu of Imperial, Mo., showed the hard-headed mentality that told the 49ers this game would be different. "Gonna be a long day ... this is the new Rams, baby!" Wittu yelled.

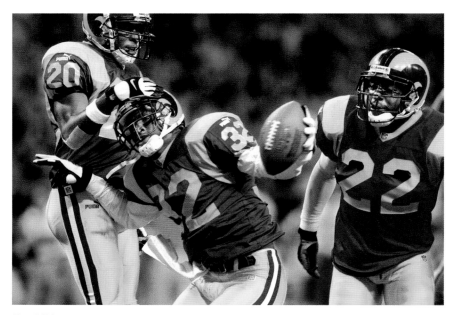

Dre' Bly (center) celebrated his fourth-quarter interception along with Taje Allen (20) and Billy Jenkins. "For five years, we used the word potential — which I don't like," safety Keith Lyle said. "Everybody's got potential. We've got playmakers."

Tony Horne ensured that the 49ers' gamelong pursuit would be futile when he ran a third-quarter kickoff back 97 yards for a touchdown. San Francisco had cut the Rams' lead to 28-20 before the runback, the first touchdown kickoff return of the season in the NFL.

	1ST	2ND	3RD	4TH	TOTAL
49ERS	3	14	3	0	20
RAMS	21	7	7	7	42

SCORING SUMMARY

QTR	TEAM	PLAY	TIME
1st	**RAMS**	TD	Bruce 13 yd. pass from Warner (Wilkins kick) 7:42
1st	**RAMS**	TD	Bruce 5 yd. pass from Warner (Wilkins kick) 4:26
1st	**49ERS**	FG	Richey 42 yds. 1:34
1st	**RAMS**	TD	Bruce 45 yd. pass from Warner (Wilkins kick) 1:12
2nd	**49ERS**	TD	Phillips 2 yd. run (Richey kick) 12:24
2nd	**RAMS**	TD	Robinson 22 yd. pass from Warner (Wilkins kick) .4:09
2nd	**49ERS**	TD	Bryant fumble recovery in end zone (Richey kick) .1:59
3rd	**49ERS**	FG	Richey 43 yds. 1:42
3rd	**RAMS**	TD	Horne 97 yd. kickoff return (Wilkins kick)............1:25
4th	**RAMS**	TD	Bruce 42 yd. pass from Warner (Wilkins kick) 11:11

OFFENSE

49ERS

PASSING	ATT	COMP	YDS	INT	TD
Jeff Garcia	36	22	233	3	0

RECEIVING	CATCHES	YDS	TD
Terrell Owens	6	60	
Charlie Garner	5	57	
J.J. Stokes	4	54	
Jerry Rice	4	42	
Lawrence Phillips	2	11	
Fred Beasley	1	9	

RUSHING	RUSHES	YDS	TD
Charlie Garner	13	52	
Lawrence Phillips	4	9	1
Jeff Garcia	1	5	
Fred Beasley	2	4	
Jerry Rice	1	2	

RAMS

PASSING	ATT	COMP	YDS	INT	TD
Kurt Warner	23	20	323	5	1

RECEIVING	CATCHES	YDS	TD
Isaac Bruce	5	134	4
Marshall Faulk	4	38	
Torry Holt	3	67	
Jeff Robinson	2	31	1
Az-Zahir Hakim	2	22	
Robert Holcombe	2	15	
James Hodgins	1	10	
Ricky Proehl	1	6	

RUSHING	RUSHES	YDS	TD
Robert Holcombe	6	47	
Justin Watson	11	46	
Kurt Warner	1	10	
Marshall Faulk	7	6	
James Hodgins	1	2	
Paul Justin	2	-2	

KEY TO THE GAME

The 49ers had chipped into the Rams' big lead and were down by 8 late in the third quarter. That's when Tony Horne took the kickoff and galloped down the left sideline for a touchdown. The play gave the Rams a 35-20 lead and ensured that the long spell the 49ers had over the Rams would be broken.

Georgia Frontiere and coach Dick Vermeil had no trouble embracing this very special victory after 17 consecutive setbacks against San Francisco.

FINAL TAKE

BY BERNIE MIKLASZ

Seeing is believing.

After they'd shown the 49ers and the world that they are for real, the Rams returned to their locker-room, a 42-20 victory in their scraped, bloodied hands.

The players formed a circle, lowered their heads and prayed. Now it was time to hand out the goodies. Rams middle line-backer London Fletcher is the personification of a Dick Vermeil player. Too small, the scouts said. Nobody wanted him. Nobody checked his heart, either, until DV noticed that all Fletcher does is play like crazy until the last running back falls.

So it was appropriate for Fletcher — who represents everything right about the new Rams — to present a game ball to Vermeil.

"It's about time," Fletcher said, "that we give a game ball to a man who brought these players and coaches together."

Remember, this was the same team that nearly rebelled against Vermeil last season. His practices were long and borderline abusive, and the offense got lost in the sideline confusion and coaching chaos. But Vermeil changed, the offense changed, the karma changed, everything changed.

So when Vermeil reached to accept the ball from Fletcher, the players erupted in applause. They love him now. Vermeil, who returned to coaching for precious moments like these, choked up as he addressed his squad.

"I've put some work in here," Vermeil said. "But you players do all the physical work. And our coaches work very hard. This is very, very meaningful to me." Vermeil in turn awarded game balls to owners Georgia Frontiere and Stan Kroenke.

"You just took my breath away," Frontiere told the Rams. "I'm the happiest person in the world, but I feel like crying."

Georgia cried. Dick cried. A few players wept, too.

Dick Vermeil helped an emotional Isaac Bruce wipe away years of frustration after his third touchdown catch, in the first quarter. "I got a little touched," Bruce said.

A HIGH FIVE IN ST. LOUIS

◇

BY JIM THOMAS

They loved LA but were loved in St. Louis.

After another season of apathy in Anaheim, the Los Angeles Rams startled the football world by moving to St. Louis in 1995.

Transplanted in the Midwest, the young Rams were strangers in a strange land. St. Louis was devoid of oceans, mountains, smog and movie stars. It was a flatland, hot in the summer and cold in the winter.

Some players had never seen snow until December 1995. Or packed football stadiums. Unlike LA, St. Louisans actually attended Rams games, win or lose.

And it was all winning early in the 1995 season. The Rams magically jumped to a 5-1 start, took the city by storm, and briefly became a national story.

"It was cool," said safety Keith Lyle. "We were Cinderella. But we blew it."

The 5-1 start deteriorated into a 7-9 season. The Rams won only six games in 1996; five games in '97; and just four games in '98. The fans began to grumble and stay away from the games. And players came and went in dizzying fashion.

"That's one of the toughest things about being a professional athlete," cornerback Todd Lyght said. "You get close to guys, and then one week they're traded, or they may get cut."

And now, with the Rams in their fifth season in St. Louis, there are just five survivors from LA: Lyle, Lyght, defensive tackle D'Marco Farr, wide receiver Isaac Bruce and defensive end Jay Williams.

"It feels good," Lyle said. "It's like you can keep throwing these challenges at us … and we're just going to stick through it."

"It's something special," Bruce said. "I enjoy being in that group. And I hope we'll be here till we retire."

All things considered, Lyght says: "I like St. Louis. I would love to finish my career here, and watch this thing get turned around. Watch this become a playoff-caliber team, and hopefully, one day win the Super Bowl."

And there's one area where LA can't hold a candle to St. Louis, in Lyght's opinion.

"St. Louis being a smaller community, and more into the traditional football vibe, that's outstanding for the team," he said. "It's better for us as players to know that the crowd is that enthusiastic about what we're doing.

"I remember my rookie season in California, we were playing the 49ers at home and 50 percent of the fans were 49er fans. We were getting beat pretty soundly. This was a home game, and the crowd was chanting, 'Beat LA!' It was crushing for me.

"But the enthusiasm we have at the TWA Dome is unlike no other. There have been times when we've dominated on defense, and the crowd gets so into it that it's almost impossible for the quarterbacks to hear their checks.

"If we can play at that level, and we can get the crowd into it and create that type of energy, the TWA Dome is going to be a hard place to come in and try to win ballgames. I think 1999 is the year that we make our big move."

Todd Lyght, one of the five "LA Rams" left on the team , was a solid force on defense all year. He corralled Tampa Bay's Mike Alstott in the playoffs.

THE MARCH THROUGH GEORGIA

◇

BY JIM THOMAS

Pretend for a moment you didn't watch the game. And don't know the score. Now, listen to coach Dick Vermeil, moments after the Rams-Falcons contest at the Georgia Dome:

"There's a lot of things we as coaches will learn from this experience. . . . I'm disappointed we didn't execute our passing game better. We all know we can do it much better. . . . Two times on the road now, we've sort of hit a lull in the ballgame. . . . We just got out of rhythm."

So, you're thinking, that the Rams:

A) Got their horns handed to them by Atlanta, **B)** Lost a nail-biter to the defending NFC champions, **C)** Won on a last-second field goal by Jeff Wilkins.

No. No. And no.

Instead, the juggernaut that is Rams Football '99 rolled to a 41-13 victory. They are off to a 5-0 start for the first time since 1989, the franchise's last playoff season.

Amazingly, they did it with their "B" game. In other words, less than their best stuff.

"It wasn't beautiful, but it was a real sound win," Vermeil said. "If it was beautiful, I don't know what the score would have been."

And that's the scary part. The Rams romped even though Kurt Warner passed for only 111 yards.

Didn't matter. Running back Marshall Faulk broke loose for 181 yards rushing, and Tony Horne raced 101 yards with a kickoff for a score.

And on three second-quarter trips into the "red zone" — inside the Rams 20 — the Falcons offense almost got outscored by the Rams defense. Grant Wistrom intercepted a deflected pass by Chris Chandler and rumbled 91 yards for a touchdown.

"Everything that we're doing, everything we're preparing for, it's working, it's clicking," safety Keith Lyle said. "Today was the first time that the offense didn't have the great game that they've been having."

But as defensive end Kevin Carter said: "It still didn't matter. This team has been beating people in every phase of the game."

Grant Wistrom got the glad hand from coach Dick Vermeil after getting his hands on a Chris Chandler pass and going 91 yards with an interception for a second-quarter touchdown.

D'Marco Farr put the squeeze on Falcons running back Ken Oxendine (center) and quarterback Chris Chandler (12) in the first quarter. The Rams built an early 14-0 lead by holding Atlanta to only 5 net yards in the quarter.

	1ST	2ND	3RD	4TH	TOTAL
RAMS	**14**	**14**	**6**	**7**	**41**
FALCONS	**0**	**10**	**0**	**3**	**13**

SCORING SUMMARY

QTR	TEAM	PLAY		TIME
1st	**RAMS**	TD	Bruce 4 yd. pass from Warner (Wilkins kick)	9:20
1st	**RAMS**	TD	Faulk 6 yd. run (Wilkins kick)	2:03
2nd	**FALCONS**	TD	Christian 13 yd. pass from Chandler (Andersen kick)	11:19
2nd	**RAMS**	TD	Horne 101 yd. kickoff return (Wilkins kick)	10:59
2nd	**RAMS**	TD	Wistrom 91 yd. interception return (Wilkins kick)	1:42
2nd	**FALCONS**	FG	Andersen 19 yds.	:32
3rd	**RAMS**	FG	Wilkins 22 yds.	12:42
3rd	**RAMS**	FG	Wilkins 49 yds.	7:26
4th	**RAMS**	TD	Holcombe 1 yd. run (Wilkins kick)	10:26
4th	**FALCONS**	FG	Andersen 25 yds.	4:25

OFFENSE

FALCONS

PASSING	ATT	COMP	YDS	INT	TD
Chris Chandler	18	10	168	1	1
Tony Graziani	18	10	126	1	0

RECEIVING	CATCHES	YDS	TD
Terance Mathis	7	75	
Reggie Kelly	3	70	
Bob Christian	3	31	1
Tim Dwight	2	56	
Ken Oxendine	2	20	
Chris Calloway	2	19	
Byron Hanspard	1	23	

RUSHING	RUSHES	YDS	TD
Ken Oxendine	8	32	
Tim Dwight	1	9	
Byron Hanspard	5	3	
Chris Chandler	2	-1	
Bob Christian	3	-2	

RAMS

PASSING	ATT	COMP	YDS	INT	TD
Kurt Warner	20	13	111	0	1

RECEIVING	CATCHES	YDS	TD
Isaac Bruce	6	48	1
Marshall Faulk	3	32	
Roland Williams	2	17	
Robert Holcombe	2	14	

RUSHING	RUSHES	YDS	TD
Marshall Faulk	18	181	1
Amp Lee	3	3	
Kurt Warner	2	3	
Robert Holcombe	5	2	1

Rams get room to run over Falcons

KEY TO THE GAME

Quarterback Chris Chandler seemed to be reviving the Falcons offense. Down 21-7, he had his team in scoring position before halftime. But on first and goal from the 9-yard line, Chandler was nailed in the backfield, and the ball fell into the hands of Grant Wistrom. Wistrom outraced the Falcons offense to give the Rams a 28-7 lead.

> *They put up a hell of a game.*
> *They did what they wanted to do, and we were at their mercy.*
> *They have a strong team.*

Falcons defensive end **Chuck Smith**

Kurt Warner didn't exactly have to dial 911 in his first visit to the Georgia Dome — a 28-point victory — but his 111-yard passing output was his lowest of the regular season.

Tony Horne's 101-yard kickoff return brought out the Rams chorus line in force in the second quarter. Horne (second from right) gets set to boogie with (from right) Dexter McCleon, Rich Coady, Dre' Bly and Troy Pelshak. For the second week in a row, Horne had reversed the momentum with a backbreaking return, giving the Rams a 21-7 lead. "Every time we hit the field, we expect it can go all the way," Horne said.

FINAL TAKE

BY BERNIE MIKLASZ

A few years ago, Marshall Faulk starred in a dazzling commercial for a shoe company. He was seen outrunning various modes of transportation, including a jet. Get Faulk into the open, and he has a chance to beat the speed of sound.

The Rams bought into the image when they gave Faulk a $45 million contract after acquiring him from the Indianapolis Colts for a couple of token draft picks. But for the early part of the season, Faulk was kept in the garage. The Rams waited for the right time to stretch him out.

Sunday at the Georgia Dome, the Faulk in the commercial became a virtual reality. Faulk had his personal Olympics through the overmatched Atlanta defense. He sprinted on dashes. He hurdled bodies. He performed brilliant gymnastic routines. He went on long-distance runs. It was a gold-medal performance.

Faulk rushed for 181 yards and a touchdown on 18 carries. He caught three passes for 32 yards, giving him 213 yards of total offense. Faulk had 21 touches, meaning he averaged 10.1 yards when the Rams put the football in his hands.

The Rams won 41-13, and Faulk's multiple-skills clinic left the Falcons so depleted of oxygen that they finally hushed up. All week, the trash-talking Falcons had insisted that the Rams were a fluke. We presume that any unresolved questions were answered by the Rams' second 28-point trashing of Atlanta in less than a month.

"Marshall was there. He wanted to run," Rams coach Dick Vermeil said. "He said before the game, 'Boys, I'm ready to take this one over.' And he did."

Isaac Bruce issued a pointed reminder that Falcons fans had gained only a temporary reprieve when he caught a pass just beyond the back line of the end zone in the first quarter. The Rev. Ike delivered the punch line to his sermon two plays later with a touchdown catch.

57

FAULK SHOWS HE'S SPECIAL

◇

BY JIM THOMAS

We can only wonder what Marshall Faulk might have accomplished had he actually felt good.

Faulk spent the night before the game in a local hospital with a combination of food poisoning and flulike symptoms. Feeling drained on game day, he made an early visit to the locker room before halftime for an IV.

But a couple of hours into the Browns game at the Trans World Dome, it was the Cleveland defense that was on life support. Faulk feasted on Brownies, piling up 200 yards of rushing and receiving in the Rams' 34-3 victory.

Faulk had 133 yards rushing, for his third 100-yard game of the season. He caught nine passes for 67 yards.

Twice, he took Kurt Warner passes to the Browns 1, on each occasion setting up TD tosses to tight end Roland Williams on the next play. And Faulk's 33-yard touchdown run early in the fourth quarter was a highlight reel of starts, stops, spins and instant acceleration. In his previous life, Faulk was a sports car.

"Marshall's unlimited," coach Dick Vermeil said. "He really is unlimited in what he can do."

Or as offensive guard Adam Timmerman put it, "Marshall, he's got that special little thing."

With NFL Commissioner Paul Tagliabue watching from owner Georgia Frontiere's luxury suite, Faulk did everything but leap tall buildings. However, after his tumultuous night out, Faulk does NOT have a restaurant recommendation for the Commish.

"I don't want to bad-mouth a restaurant or anything like that," Faulk said. "I'm not sure what I had. The doctors don't even know what I had. Don't want to give it a name. I don't want to see it again."

Nor do the Browns want to see Faulk again.

Roland Williams (86) had five catches for 50 yards in the rout of the Browns, and with the tight end now getting more into the act, opponents were advised that there was a new sibling among the Warner Bros.

Roland Williams celebrated the first of his two touchdown catches. "I'm happy that Roland got into the end zone a couple of times. Now, I'm just waiting to see who it's going to be next week," Kurt Warner said.

D'Marco Farr (75) put the heat on Browns quarterback Tim Couch in the second quarter. The Rams' pressure helped result in two interceptions of Couch passes.

OFFENSE

BROWNS

PASSING	ATT	COMP	YDS	INT	TD
Tim Couch	40	22	185	2	0

RECEIVING	CATCHES	YDS	TD
Leslie Shepherd	6	85	
Terry Kirby	6	18	
Kevin Johnson	3	35	
Irv Smith	3	31	
Karim Abdul-Jabbar	2	8	
Marc Edwards	2	8	

RUSHING	RUSHES	YDS	TD
Tim Couch	2	50	
Karim Abdul-Jabbar	6	27	
Terry Kirby	6	12	
Leslie Shepherd	1	5	

RAMS

PASSING	ATT	COMP	YDS	INT	TD
Kurt Warner	29	23	203	0	3
Paul Justin	5	4	25	0	0

RECEIVING	CATCHES	YDS	TD
Marshall Faulk	9	67	
Roland Williams	5	50	2
Ricky Proehl	5	29	
Isaac Bruce	4	44	1
Torry Holt	2	24	
Hodgins	2	14	

RUSHING	RUSHES	YDS	TD
Marshall Faulk	16	133	1
Justin Watson	9	69	
Isaac Bruce	1	6	
Torry Holt	1	5	
Joe Germaine	2	-2	

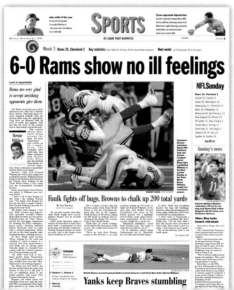

	1ST	2ND	3RD	4TH	TOTAL
BROWNS	3	0	0	0	3
RAMS	14	7	3	10	34

SCORING SUMMARY

QTR	TEAM	PLAY		TIME
1st	**RAMS**	TD	Williams 1 yd. pass from Warner (Wilkins kick)	8:34
1st	**RAMS**	TD	Bruce 4 yd. pass from Warner (Wilkins kick)	6:49
1st	**BROWNS**	FG	Dawson 47 yds.	:17
2nd	**RAMS**	TD	Williams 1 yd. pass from Warner (Wilkins kick)	10:59
3rd	**RAMS**	FG	Wilkins 28 yds.	3:13
4th	**RAMS**	TD	Faulk 33 yd. run (Wilkins kick)	14:50
4th	**RAMS**	FG	Wilkins 36 yds.	4:06

KEY TO THE GAME

The Rams built a 14-0 lead before the Browns offense took the field. After a Roland Williams touchdown grab, the Rams kickoff team recovered a fumble. Four plays later, Kurt Warner completed a 4-yard touchdown pass to Isaac Bruce, putting the Browns in a deep hole.

"*Marshall Faulk killed us by himself.*"
Browns safety **Corey Fuller**

London Fletcher grabbed the hands of fans after grabbing Browns ballcarriers all day. Fletcher finished with a team-leading seven tackles and two assists and made it his personal mission to make Browns rookie receiver Kevin Johnson eat his words. Johnson had "guaranteed" victory for the Browns. "The only thing he was guaranteeing was a butt-kicking for his team," Fletcher said.

Isaac Bruce dived to the turf to snare a first-quarter touchdown pass as the Rams put the Browns down for the count early, taking a 14-0 lead before Cleveland had run a play from scrimmage.

1 2 3 4 5 6 7 8 9 10 11 12 13 14 15 16

GAME

6

OCT. 24, 1999
TRANS WORLD DOME

RAMS 34
BROWNS 3

FINAL TAKE

By Bernie Miklasz

The Rams are living up to their nickname now. They are a Warner Bros. cartoon. They play noisy, colorful, slapstick football. They set devious little traps for opponents. They blow up defenses with all sorts of tricks and gadgets. And just like the stars of the cartoon shows, they always win in the end.

The coyote chases Marshall Faulk around the field. He goes beep-beep and scoots in for a touchdown. The varmints can't catch him. And when explosive wide receiver Isaac Bruce gets the football in his hands, it's virtual dynamite.

Sunday, tight end Roland Williams got a turn and caught two touchdown passes. Williams joined Faulk as the featured attractions in the Warner Bros. matinee at the Trans World Dome, a 34-3 romp over the overmatched Cleveland Browns.

The Rams were missing a few toys. Wide receiver and punt-return specialist Az-Zahir Hakim didn't play because of a sore groin. Kickoff-return jet Tony Horne started his four-game suspension for violating the NFL's substance-abuse policy. Starting fullback Robert Holcombe went out early with a strained hamstring. Bruce left late in the third quarter after twisting his knee (nothing serious). No fear. Faulk rushed for 133 yards and caught 67 yards in passes in a clinical 200-yard performance.

Skeptics can whine about soft schedules from now until NFL Commissioner Paul Tagliabue returns to St. Louis, but the Rams have won their six games by an average score of 36-10. It's one thing to be winning on a tipped pass here or a field goal there. But the Rams are destroying teams. Don't dare arrive late to Rams games or you might miss the turning point: the coin flip.

Todd Gauthier, a resident of Phoenix, attended his first Rams game and showed his special way of helping them get a leg up on the Browns.

ONE WAY: ATTACK, ATTACK, ATTACK

◇

By Bernie Miklasz
and Jim Thomas

It happens every autumn. A National Football League assistant coach, leading a life of relative obscurity, suddenly is discovered. He's heralded as a hot new head-coaching prospect. Excitable NFL pundits go on television to praise the coach for reinventing the game.

Rams offensive coordinator Mike Martz is the instant genius this season. He's getting rave reviews — deservedly so — for running his updated version of the Don Coryell passing game.

In a conservative NFL, the other 30 teams are scoring about 20 points a game. The Rams averaged nearly 33 points per game in the regular season. They have fun. They line up in crazy formations. They run deceptive plays. They attack. The Rams have added a swirl of flavor to a vanilla NFL.

And hype is at Martz's door, pounding loudly, demanding to be let in. Martz, a dignified man, is inclined to hide under his desk. If anything, he rejects credit.

"It's the players," he said. "I've been in the situation where you call plays but you don't have good players. So, the plays don't matter much. But when you have good players, all of a sudden, you become smart. The plays work when you have good players. And we have a lot of good players. It's as simple as that."

Almost as intimidating as the Rams' array of offensive personnel is their play-calling. And it goes beyond merely the "attack-mode" premise of the system. Martz has a seemingly bottomless bag of tricks in his playbook.

Shovel passes. ... Option pitches from Az-Zahir Hakim. ... Reverses and fake-reverses. ... Halfback passes. ... And all sorts of strange formations and alignments.

Martz loves it. The players love it. The fans love it. And you know what? Owner Georgia Frontiere loves it, too.

"That's why our guys play fast, because I think they're having fun," Martz said. "It's kind of an attitude that they take towards how they play. It's entertaining, sure.

"But when you have the athletes that we have, you have to move them around and get them out on the perimeter. The worst thing we can do is bunch them all in the I-formation, and let them zero in on you. But like I said, this would take on a whole different meaning with lesser players."

The conventional wisdom on the Rams was that after a month or so of the season, the rest of the league would get a book on Martz, the new coordinator, and Kurt Warner, the new quarterback. But it just hasn't happened.

"The whole philosophy of what we do is that we want to dictate and take control of the game, and not let the defense do that," Martz said. "I guess the thing that happens with all coaches in this league, and players too, is you get to the point sometimes where you tighten up a little bit, especially in big games.

"You just can't play this game tight. You've just got to let it all hang out and not worry about it. If you go after teams like that, you always keep the defense on its heels. Especially when you have the players that we have. It's easy to be aggressive."

THROWN FOR A LOSS

— ◇ —

BY JIM THOMAS

Jeff Wilkins saw the ball veering right but hoped it would straighten out. Then, he went down in an instant — as did a heretofore perfect Rams season.

On his back, Wilkins couldn't see the result of his 38-yard field-goal try. But he heard it, heard the crowd going bonkers because the kick barely missed wide right with 7 seconds remaining.

Tennessee escaped with a 24-21 victory in front of a franchise-record crowd of 66,415 at Adelphia Coliseum.

"I would have bet my house (Wilkins' kick) was good," Rams defensive tackle D'Marco Farr said. "From where I was sitting, it looked like it was good. I can't even describe the feeling when I saw those arms wave 'no good.' It felt like all the air just got sucked out of the place."

The visitors from St. Louis fell victim to a Rams-like barrage in the first quarter as the Titans (6-1) took advantage of two turnovers to take a 21-0 lead only 13 1/2 minutes into the game.

Quarterback Kurt Warner, despite throwing for 328 yards and three TDs, fumbled four times. Two were recovered by the Titans deep in Rams territory and were converted into Tennessee touchdowns.

And then, there was Rams offensive tackle Fred Miller. He struggled mightily with the crowd noise and Titans defensive end Jevon Kearse. Miller was called for an astounding six false starts and two holding penalties.

"He lost his composure completely," coach Dick Vermeil said.

The Rams picked themselves up, regrouped at halftime and nearly pulled off a heart-stopping comeback before heading back to St. Louis with a 6-1 record. They are invincible no more.

"I hate losing," safety Keith Lyle said. "You kind of want to crawl into the airplane and not let anybody see you. But you've got to deal with it."

Fred Miller spent much of his day staring at the zebras. Confronted by lightning-quick defensive end Jevon Kearse and a roaring Adelphia Coliseum crowd, the Rams right tackle had six false starts and two holding penalties, one of which was declined.

Ricky Proehl caught a pass as well as some abuse from Tennessee's Samari Rolle (21). Proehl had four catches for 45 yards and in the final seconds was stopped just short of a first down before the Rams' attempt at a tying field goal.

Az-Zahir Hakim exited the Adelphia Coliseum field after his first taste of defeat in the '99 season.

Kurt Warner disappeared under some Titanic blitzes in the first half. But despite being sacked six times and fumbling four times, he came back to complete 29 of 46 for 328 yards.

	1ST	2ND	3RD	4TH	TOTAL
RAMS	0	0	14	7	21
TITANS	21	0	3	0	24

KEY TO THE GAME

The Rams staged a near-miracle comeback from a 21-0 deficit. Without timeouts and the Rams down 24-21, Kurt Warner drove the Rams to the Titans 19. A 38-yard, field-goal try by Jeff Wilkins missed wide right with seven seconds to play, and the Rams were handed their first loss.

SCORING SUMMARY

QTR	TEAM		PLAY	TIME
1st	**TITANS**	TD	Neal 1 yd. pass from McNair (Del Greco kick)	8:28
1st	**TITANS**	TD	George 17 yd. pass from McNair (Del Greco kick)	2:41
1st	**TITANS**	TD	McNair 10 yd. run (Del Greco kick)	1:24
3rd	**RAMS**	TD	Faulk 57 yd. pass from Warner (Wilkins kick)	14:33
3rd	**RAMS**	TD	Bruce 3 yd. pass from Warner (Wilkins kick)	7:55
3rd	**TITANS**	FG	Del Greco 27 yds.	4:18
4th	**RAMS**	TD	Lee 15 yd. pass from Warner (Wilkins kick)	2:14

OFFENSE

TITANS

PASSING	ATT	COMP	YDS	INT	TD
Steve McNair	29	13	186	0	2

RECEIVING	CATCHES	YDS	TD
Jackie Harris	3	44	
Eddie George	3	35	1
Yancey Thigpen	2	49	
Frank Wycheck	2	38	
Kevin Dyson	2	19	
Lorenzo Neal	1	1	1

RUSHING	RUSHES	YDS	TD
Eddie George	17	68	
Steve McNair	12	36	1
Rodney Thomas	2	-1	

RAMS

PASSING	ATT	COMP	YDS	INT	TD
Kurt Warner	46	29	328	0	3

RECEIVING	CATCHES	YDS	TD
Marshall Faulk	6	94	1
Isaac Bruce	6	53	1
Az-Zahir Hakim	5	62	
Torry Holt	5	55	
Ricky Proehl	4	45	
Amp Lee	1	15	1
Roland Williams	1	4	
James Hodgins	1	0	

RUSHING	RUSHES	YDS	TD
Marshall Faulk	16	90	
Kurt Warner	2	22	
Az-Zahir Hakim	1	16	

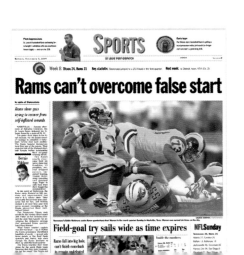

> *The Titans are a good football team, but we're better.*
> *Look at all the penalties and errors we made,*
> *and we're in the ballgame until the last play.*

Rams defensive end **Grant Wistrom**

Jeff Wilkins watched his attempt for the game-tying field goal from 38 yards that was . . . up, up . . . and wide right. Tennessee's Terry Killens ran into Wilkins on the play, but the officials ruled that Killens had been blocked into the Rams kicker, who missed for the first time in the '99 season.

GAME 7
OCT. 31, 1999
ADELPHIA COLISEUM, NASHVILLE, TENN.
TITANS 24
RAMS 21

1 2 3 4 5 6 8 9 10 11 12 13 14 15 16

FINAL TAKE

BY BERNIE MIKLASZ

Sunday afternoon at Adelphia Coliseum, the St. Louis Rams defeated the St. Louis Rams by a score of 24-21.

The game went down to the final seconds, but the Rams couldn't manage to complete a comeback victory over each other. The Rams handed themselves their first loss of the season. They were the talk of the NFL before terminating their six-game winning streak.

The Rams nearly overcame their six sacks, three lost fumbles, 15 penalties, several dropped passes, impaired hearing, sloppy third-down execution and general stage fright to rally from their staggering incompetence.

In the spirit of Halloween, the Rams came dressed in full costume and impersonated last year's 4-12 clown show. They eventually found their true character, but too late. Jeff

Wilkins missed a 38-yard field goal with seven seconds left as the Rams preserved their well-earned failure.

The Tennessee Titans took credit for the victory. Head coach Jeff Fisher all but declared himself the next Tom Landry for developing the defensive strategy that pressured Rams quarterback Kurt Warner.

What Fisher couldn't explain was how his team — up 21-0 after the Rams generously distributed handfuls of candy — scored only three points in the final three quarters and barely hung on to win.

We'd been hearing the Rams say for weeks that they could lose only by beating themselves, and Sunday, it came true. Given the circumstances, the Rams could have easily packed it in early and headed for the showers. But this is a sturdy, resilient team.

Rams players prepared to enter the grounds where their 6-0 start would be laid to rest.

71

1234567 8 9 10 11 12 13 14 15 16

GAME

8

NOV. 7, 1999
PONTIAC SILVERDOME, DETROIT
LIONS 31
RAMS 27

FUEL FOR THE SKEPTICS

◇

BY JIM THOMAS

The Fat Lady wasn't singing, but she had cleared her throat and stepped to the microphone.

D'Marco Farr had just busted through the Detroit line and thrown Gus Frerotte to the turf like a Beanie Baby. That quarterback sack, the sixth of the day by the Rams, left the Lions in a hopeless fourth-down predicament on their 21-yard line with just 1 minute 17 seconds to play.

It was over, folks. After hitting a speed bump in Tennessee, the Rams had regained the magic. They were on the verge of an inspiring 27-24 victory, and all 73,224 spectators in the Silverdome knew it.

"People started leaving, and we started unbuckling," Rams wide receiver Isaac Bruce said. "It was time to go home."

But no. On fourth and 26, Detroit quarterback Gus Frerotte threw deep. Incredibly, Lions wide receiver Germane Crowell got wide open behind Rams cornerback Dexter McCleon for a 57-yard gain. Just like that, the Lions were on the Rams 22 with one minute to play.

It gets worse. Four plays later, the Lions were in the end zone on a 12-yard pass from Frerotte to Johnnie Morton with 28 seconds to play.

In the blink of an eye, a come-from-behind victory disintegrated into a staggering 31-27 loss for the Rams.

"We had a shot to win it, we had it locked (up) and we let them get in," Farr said. "This is such an emotional loss. ... It's shocking."

As wrenching as the 24-21 loss was in Tennessee, this was twice that. No, make it five times that. Farr, for one, has never seen anything quite like it. "Maybe in John Madden Sega football," Farr said. "Fourth and 26 — you never see that."

McCleon took full responsibility.

"It was my fault," McCleon said. "I blew the play. I'm just supposed to stay deep. I let him get behind me. Basically, I let the team down, I let the fans down, I let the city of St. Louis down."

Taje Allen looked on after being victimized for Johnnie Morton's last-minute touchdown that brought the Rams to their knees.

Marshall Faulk (28) couldn't maneuver the Rams' ground game past the Detroit roadblocks. Faulk had 78 yards in receptions but just 15 yards on 11 carries as the Rams were held to only 57 yards rushing.

Kurt Warner watched a completion to Marshall Faulk from under the rush of the Lions' Tracy Scroggins. Warner saw his streak of 133 passes without an interception end. It was the third-longest such streak in franchise history.

	1ST	2ND	3RD	4TH	TOTAL
RAMS	2	10	0	15	27
LIONS	0	10	11	10	31

SCORING SUMMARY

QTR	TEAM	PLAY	TIME
1st	**RAMS**	SFT	Hill tackled by Fletcher in end zone 6:58
2nd	**LIONS**	TD	Crowell 4 yd. pass from Batch (Hanson kick)......14:19
2nd	**RAMS**	TD	Robinson 6 yd. pass from Warner (Wilkins kick) .11:32
2nd	**LIONS**	FG	Hanson 29 yds. 6:51
2nd	**RAMS**	FG	Wilkins 34 yds. ....:41
3rd	**LIONS**	TD	Schlesinger 3 yd. pass from Frerotte (2 pt. conversion: Crowell pass from Frerotte) 9:20
3rd	**LIONS**	FG	Hanson 43 yds. 4:49
4th	**RAMS**	TD	Hakim 75 yd. pass from Warner (Wilkins kick) ...10:06
4th	**LIONS**	FG	Hanson 44 yds. 6:10
4th	**RAMS**	TD	Tucker 2 yd. pass from Warner (2 pt. conversion: Bruce pass from Warner) 2:42
4th	**LIONS**	TD	Morton 12 yd. pass from Frerotte (Hanson kick) .....:28

OFFENSE

LIONS

PASSING	ATT	COMP	YDS	INT	TD
Charlie Batch	20	10	148	0	1
Gus Frerotte	16	12	209	0	2

RECEIVING	CATCHES	YDS	TD
Germane Crowell	8	163	1
Sedrick Irvin	4	65	
Johnnie Morton	4	59	1
Brian Stablein	2	48	
Pete Chryplewicz	2	18	
Cory Schlesinger	1	3	1
David Sloan	1	1	

RUSHING	RUSHES	YDS	TD
Sedrick Irvin	4	10	
Gus Frerotte	5	8	
Greg Hill	11	3	
Charlie Batch	1	3	

RAMS

PASSING	ATT	COMP	YDS	INT	TD
Kurt Warner	42	25	305	2	3
Marshall Faulk	1	0	0	0	0

RECEIVING	CATCHES	YDS	TD
Marshall Faulk	10	78	
Ricky Proehl	4	36	
Torry Holt	3	31	
Az-Zahir Hakim	2	94	1
Isaac Bruce	2	34	
Roland Williams	1	15	
Amp Lee	1	9	
Jeff Robinson	1	6	1
Ryan Tucker	1	2	1

RUSHING	RUSHES	YDS	TD
Kurt Warner	3	26	
Robert Holcombe	2	16	
Marshall Faulk	11	15	

KEY TO THE GAME

With time running out and his team trailing, Detroit's Gus Frerotte completed a fourth-and-26 desperation pass to Germane Crowell behind cornerback Dexter McCleon. The pass enabled the Lions to drive for the winning touchdown. McCleon said: "I just got caught looking back at the quarterback and I lost sight of him."

75

" We have to regroup. We're still 6-2, but I just feel like we're just an everyday 6-2 team now. "

Rams safety **Keith Lyle**

Isaac Bruce had a third-quarter reception on his fingertips, but the Lions' Terry Fair moved in to break up the play. Bruce was held to two catches for 34 yards.

1234567 8 01112131415 16

GAME
NOV. 7, 1999
PONTIAC SILVERDOME, DETROIT

LIONS 31
RAMS 27

FINAL TAKE

By Bernie Miklasz

Halfway through their season, the Rams are 6-2. That's a good record, better than anyone could have predicted or hoped for before the 1999 season.

Still, the question must be asked: Is this a good team?

I honestly don't know the answer. The Rams obviously have some outstanding components and can win a lot of games in the final eight weeks. The Rams are fortunate to be competing in the weak, meek NFC West — easily the worst division in the NFL.

That tends to distort reality, but if we look at this objectively, the truth is that the Rams have flunked their only two tests against quality opponents.

The Rams, all but shivering in a hostile stadium, melted under pressure early on in the 24-21 loss at Tennessee. And on Sunday, they collapsed late in a disgusting, inexcusable, 31-27 defeat to the Detroit Lions.

I'm sorry. I can't rationalize this loss. Top teams just shouldn't lose games like this.

The 6-0 start wasn't a mirage, but the last two Sundays have been disturbing. So, what do we really have here? It's tricky because we might not know the Rams' true value until the playoffs. Assuming, of course, that the Rams still qualify for the postseason. Mere competence should take care of that.

Sunday's loss was one of those potentially devastating blows that could blast a hole through the team's confidence. The Rams couldn't stop a Fourth and Impossible, and you can only hope that they'll limit the emotional damage.

I asked cornerback Todd Lyght: Is this a confident 6-2 team or a fragile 6-2 team?

"I don't know at this point," Lyght said.

We don't know, either.

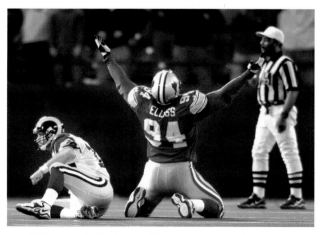

Kurt Warner (left) absorbed the impact upon throwing a last-gasp interception in the final seconds, after the Rams had let the lead slip away.

THE STYLE CHANGES; THE MAN DOESN'T

———— ◇ ————

BY BERNIE MIKLASZ

Every now and then at Dick Vermeil's weekly news conference, a TV sportscaster tries to score points by giving the coach an opportunity to lash out at those who criticized DV during 1997 and '98, when the Rams lost 23 of 32 games.

Vermeil, one of the truly good guys in his business, has too much class to berate those who have jumped him in the past. But his coaching ego does flare up on occasion.

"I never really took any of those (negative) kind of evaluations seriously," Vermeil said. "As I've said before, whatever you write is fine, but just be willing to take it back someday. Because we'll get this thing turned around."

Vermeil has turned around the Rams; he has done a sensational job this season. But with apologies to Vermeil, there's no reason to try to revise history by taking back anything that has been written previously.

Vermeil was an ineffective coach in 1997 and '98. He coddled underachievers (Tony Banks) but publicly ripped into his most dedicated players (Isaac Bruce). DV was a sucker for con artists (Lawrence Phillips). He misjudged personnel, choosing to start mediocre players ahead of those who could make a positive impact (rookies Grant Wistrom and Az-Zahir Hakim largely were wasted last year).

Vermeil was loyal to a fault; several hours before the Rams were about to announce the signing of free-agent quarterback Trent Green, Vermeil hesitated and decided to stick with Banks — only to change his mind again.

Vermeil's offense had no real plan, no real identity. For a time, he wanted to call the plays but couldn't get them into the huddle on time. His sideline demeanor created chaos. He also worked his players into the ground, wearing out their legs.

Vermeil's player relations were strained; several players blew off Vermeil's final team meeting after the 1998 season. Just a total mess.

There was a natural reason for this turmoil. Vermeil was away from coaching for 14 years and painfully struggled to adapt after re-entering the profession.

But he has adjusted. And that's why Vermeil deserves immense respect for what he has been able to accomplish — not only with his team but also with himself. Vermeil turned around a losing program only after realizing that he had to turn himself around.

The belief that he has changed, Vermeil said, "is an abused issue."

Actually, it's a fascinating issue. Why doesn't Vermeil take credit and accept praise for boldly doing what needed to be done? This man reinvented his team during one offseason.

Vermeil hired Mike Martz to run the offense, and Vermeil has stayed out of Martz's way. DV ran off mediocre players and troublemakers. He upgraded the offense with the additions of halfback Marshall Faulk, guard Adam Timmerman and wideout Torry Holt.

Vermeil's player relations have improved. He cut back in training camp and accepted a plan to save Bruce's hamstrings by limiting his repetitions. The morale is way up. Vermeil also held his team together when the players were shaken emotionally by Green's season-ending knee injury.

It's all working. Vermeil has gone from bad coach to outstanding coach, a remarkable transformation. He saved himself — and the Rams.

GAME
9
NOV. 14, 1999
TRANS WORLD DOME
RAMS 35
PANTHERS 10

FLYING AGAIN IN THE DOME

◇

BY JIM THOMAS

Big crowd. Big plays. Big score.

The 35-10 victory over Carolina seemed like old times for the Rams at the Trans World Dome. The Rams have won six straight at the Dome, including all five played here this season. The average score of those five? Why ... 35-10.

"It was important to get things going again like we had earlier in the year," quarterback Kurt Warner said. "Get a big victory. Get back home. Get the fans excited again."

After wrenching road losses before hostile crowds in Tennessee and Detroit, the sound of 65,965 screaming fans at the Dome was music to the ears of the Rams.

"If you go the other way and drop another one today, that really hurts your confidence," said guard Adam Timmerman, part of a Rams offensive line that kept Warner unsacked. "We came in and handled it very well, coming off the losses."

Warner said: "This is where we want to be at the end of the year. We want to play our games here at home because we do have such a distinct advantage."

That's "games" — as in playoff games. The Rams' victory enabled them to regain the lead for home-field advantage in the playoffs.

"Our fans in St. Louis are just incredible," said defensive end Kevin Carter. "We looked forward to coming back here and establishing ourselves as one of the top teams in the NFC."

Despite all that "coach-speak" about taking them one at a time, don't think coach Dick Vermeil isn't starting to think playoffs. Why else was the entire first-team offense still on the field when Marshall Faulk scored the game's final TD on an 18-yard run with a mere 71 seconds to play?

"We're no longer undefeated," Vermeil said. "We're in an NFC division where other teams are winning. Once we qualify for the playoffs, then there's some other categories that we have to be aware of, that's the total point factor and everything else."

Roland Williams tumbled into the corner of the end zone on a 19-yard TD pass from Kurt Warner in the second quarter.

Kevin Carter, who bagged 2¹/₂ more sacks on the way to the league sack title, took down Panthers quarterback Steve Beuerlein for a 7-yard loss in the second quarter. Carter was named NFC defensive player of the week.

	1ST	2ND	3RD	4TH	TOTAL
PANTHERS	7	3	0	0	10
RAMS	14	7	7	7	35

SCORING SUMMARY

QTR	TEAM	PLAY		TIME
1st	**PANTHERS**	TD	Walls 14 yd. pass from Beuerlein (Kasay kick)	9:38
1st	**RAMS**	TD	Bruce 22 yd. pass from Warner (Wilkins kick)	7:02
1st	**RAMS**	TD	Lyght 57 yd. interception return (Wilkins kick)	:15
2nd	**RAMS**	TD	Williams 19 yd. pass from Warner (Wilkins kick)	5:31
2nd	**PANTHERS**	FG	Kasay 24 yds.	:44
3rd	**RAMS**	TD	M.Jones 37 yd. fumble return (Wilkins kick)	11:25
4th	**RAMS**	TD	Faulk 18 yd. run (Wilkins kick)	1:11

Keith Lyle broke up a pass but suffered a bruised nerve in his shoulder. He returned in time for the playoffs. "I prayed to God every day to heal me, and he did," Lyle later said.

OFFENSE

PANTHERS

PASSING	ATT	COMP	YDS	INT	TD
Steve Beuerlein	39	24	286	2	1

RECEIVING	CATCHES	YDS	TD
Muhsin Muhammad	9	125	
Wesley Walls	5	54	1
Patrick Jeffers	3	43	
William Floyd	3	31	
Fred Lane	3	9	
Donald Hayes	1	24	

RUSHING	RUSHES	YDS	TD
Fred Lane	13	54	
Anthony Johnson	2	29	
Steve Beuerlein	3	20	
William Floyd	5	14	

RAMS

PASSING	ATT	COMP	YDS	INT	TD
Kurt Warner	29	19	283	1	2

RECEIVING	CATCHES	YDS	TD
Isaac Bruce	5	69	1
Roland Williams	3	38	1
Marshall Faulk	2	64	
Robert Holcombe	2	45	
Ricky Proehl	2	18	
Torry Holt	2	16	
Jeff Robinson	1	30	
Az-Zahir Hakim	1	5	
Amp Lee	1	-2	

RUSHING	RUSHES	YDS	TD
Marshall Faulk	16	73	
Robert Holcombe	2	4	
Kurt Warner	1	2	
Az-Zahir Hakim	1	0	

KEY TO THE GAME

Carolina quarterback Steve Beuerlein completed his first nine passes. The 10th was caught too, but by Rams safety Todd Lyght. With just 15 seconds to play in the first quarter, Lyght sealed off receiver Patrick Jeffers, stepped in front of a pass and ran it back 57 yards for a touchdown. That gave the Rams a 14-7 lead and energized the Dome crowd.

"Nobody has a higher standard than we do in this room."

Kurt Warner

Dexter McCleon (left) moved in to break up a second-quarter pass intended for Carolina's Donald Hayes.

FINAL TAKE

BY BERNIE MIKLASZ

What's wrong with the Rams? That 6-0 start is a memory now. It isn't the same.

Carolina marched down the field for a touchdown on the opening drive. The Rams couldn't run the football. They dropped passes. The offense stagnated.

No one on the Rams offensive line could block defensive tackle Sean Gilbert. No one in the secondary could put the adhesive on Carolina wide receiver Muhsin Muhammad.

And then, there's Kurt Warner. His QB rating for the game was only 106. He's slipping. When will Trent Green be ready? Marshall Faulk had only 15 yards rushing on his first 11 carries; no wonder he's getting ripped by rational-minded sports fans in letters to the editor.

After the game, Rams coach Dick Vermeil walked into the interview room, bit off his words, and stressed the need for his team to do better.

Oh, and by the way, the Rams trampled the Pan-thers 35-10 and raised their record to an NFC-best 7-2. But I found it interesting — hence, the sarcasm — that the players and coaches were so blase and generally unsatisfied about their performance.

During the game, Vermeil barked at players and slammed his clipboard to the turf on one occasion. DV sprinkled his postgame comments with criticism, condemning the Rams' running game.

Let's call a timeout. Vermeil spoke for many of us when he said, "I'm actually a little spoiled."

The Rams have spoiled us. And ain't it fun to be greedy?

"It's been a long process," D'Marco Farr said. "There were all those Sundays when we were so desperate, just begging someone to make a play or do anything positive. Now, it's like, 'The offense should score every time.' And, 'The defense shouldn't give up a scoring drive.' We've come a long way."

Kevin Carter helped restore the roar from Rams fans with another of his league-leading 17 sacks.

85

YOU CAN TAKE AWAY THE 'LOSER' LABEL

◇

BY JIM THOMAS

They are losers no more.

Marshall Faulk could fall through a trap door. Isaac Bruce could be kidnapped by aliens, never to be seen again. Kurt Warner could start playing like an Arena league quarterback. Check that. Kurt Warner could start playing like a bad Arena league quarterback.

That and more could cause the Rams to lose all six of their remaining regular-season games. But with eight victories after a 23-7 triumph over San Francisco, the Rams are incapable of having a losing season.

It is mathematically impossible. The absolute worst they can finish is 8-8. For the first time since 1989, the Rams won't have a losing season.

"We shut it down," said cornerback Todd Lyght, who has been a Ram for eight of those nine straight losing seasons. "It's a beautiful thing. In the NFL I've never been in a situation where I had more than seven wins. And

to be sitting at Game 10 with eight wins — and six to play — it's just hard to put into words, in all honesty."

The Rams had only their "B" game on offense, maybe even their "C" game. Warner completed "only" 22 of 40 passes, his worst game of the season in terms of accuracy.

But for the second week in a row, the Rams defense roared. There were seven sacks, including two by Kevin Carter. St. Louis came up with five turnovers, including an interception return for a TD by linebacker Mike Jones.

Jones — designated a game-day captain by Vermeil — handed game balls to Lyght and Bruce.

"Todd's been here the longest, and Isaac's been here the longest on offense," Jones said. "The 49ers have been sweeping us for so many years, I thought that of all the people who have been here, they deserved the game balls."

Torry Holt couldn't corral this first-quarter pass in the face of coverage from Monty Montgomery (24). But the Rams, after a sluggish beginning, methodically put away the 49ers.

Fred Miller (left) knew that things were definitely looking up after the Rams had completed their first sweep of the 49ers since 1980. D'Marco Farr had called 3Com Park "an evil place for the Rams." Todd Lyght said: "It's official now. We're the cream team of the NFC West. If anybody wants a shot at this thing, they've got to come see us. They've got to come to St. Louis."

Kurt Warner set his sights downfield, and the presence of Orlando Pace gave him time to enjoy the view, a familiar theme in the '99 Super Bowl run.

	1ST	2ND	3RD	4TH	TOTAL
RAMS	3	10	10	0	23
49ERS	0	7	0	0	7

SCORING SUMMARY

QTR	TEAM	PLAY		TIME
1st	**RAMS**	FG	Wilkins 40 yds.	4:47
2nd	**49ERS**	TD	Beasley 1 yd. run (Richey kick)	8:13
2nd	**RAMS**	TD	Bruce 5 yd. pass from Warner (Wilkins kick)	3:02
2nd	**RAMS**	FG	Wilkins 20 yds.	0:00
3rd	**RAMS**	TD	M. Jones 44 yd. interception return (Wilkins kick)	9:41
3rd	**RAMS**	FG	Wilkins 49 yds.	2:23

OFFENSE

49ERS

PASSING	ATT	COMP	YDS	INT	TD
Jeff Garcia	15	8	89	2	0
Steve Stenstrom	12	7	108	1	0

RECEIVING	CATCHES	YDS	TD
Terrell Owens	6	120	
Fred Beasley	3	25	
Jerry Rice	3	23	
Greg Clark	2	22	
J.J. Stokes	1	7	

RUSHING	RUSHES	YDS	TD
Charlie Garner	16	77	
Fred Beasley	4	16	1
Jeff Garcia	4	13	
Steve Stenstrom	1	0	

RAMS

PASSING	ATT	COMP	YDS	INT	TD
Kurt Warner	40	22	201	1	1

RECEIVING	CATCHES	YDS	TD
Isaac Bruce	11	93	1
Marshall Faulk	4	43	
Torry Holt	3	25	
Az-Zahir Hakim	2	32	
Chris Thomas	1	6	
Roland Williams	1	2	

RUSHING	RUSHES	YDS	TD
Marshall Faulk	21	126	
Robert Holcombe	5	16	
Kurt Warner	2	12	
Torry Holt	1	6	
Isaac Bruce	1	4	

KEY TO THE GAME

Trailing 13-7, the 49ers were driving to take the lead midway through the third quarter. That's when defensive tackle D'Marco Farr tipped a pass and sent it wobbling into the arms of Mike Jones. Jones, a former running back at Missouri, broke a tackle and outraced several 49ers on the way to the end zone.

" The best thing about it, even better than sweeping them, was the 'Niners players coming up to tell us, 'You guys are really good' ... It's awesome to be validated like that by the 49ers. "

Rams defensive tackle **D'Marco Farr**

Grant Wistrom jumped for joy after putting 49ers quarterback Steve Stenstrom on the turf in the first quarter.

FINAL TAKE

By Bernie Miklasz

Same old 'Niners? Wrong.

"They're the new 'Niners," Rams cornerback Todd Lyght said. "The brand-new 'Niners. And I love them, because they just can't get it done."

What, you expected humility?

After winning 23-7 and picking over the carcass that is the San Francisco 49ers, the Rams would not permit an eruption of good manners. Not after having spent so many years getting their faces pushed down into the mud by the 49ers at Candlestick Park, or 3Com Park, or 3Win Park — whatever they're calling the windy, hideous stadium these days.

Not after losing approximately 379 consecutive games to the 49ers before breaking free from the chains earlier this season. Not after coming to San Francisco all these years to get flattened by a cable car, rolled down the Lombard Street hill, bopped over the head with a loaf of stale sourdough and dumped onto Alcatraz Island.

The Rams completed their first season sweep over the 49ers since 1980. They won here for the first time since 1990. And to the Rams players, it did not matter that the 49ers were a butterfly without wings, or a team with no quarterback.

This was a pathetic San Francisco squad that the Rams dragged through three hours of dull grime and punishment. The 49ers are a ghost ship now. When you come to San Francisco for a Rams-49ers game, the most difficult challenge is booking a decent restaurant reservation on Saturday night.

The Silence of the Lambs officially came to an end when the Rams sprinted off the field. Rams fans shouted their encouragement. Bitter 49ers fans screamed their disdain. Rams players hollered back.

"Get used to it," defensive tackle Ray Agnew said, speaking to fans of both teams.

Grant Wistrom knew that back-to-back victories over the 49ers was sweep success. The Rams defensive end roamed the sideline saying, 'Who brought the broom, baby?'

CHISELED OUT OF A BLOCK OF ICE

—◇—

By Elizabethe Holland

Kevin Carter's eyes narrow, then widen. His shoulders tense, his speech quickens. He's trying to describe what it's like to zero in on a quarterback, the piece of meat defensive linemen everywhere dream about.

The flashbacks are intense. And Carter has plenty — an NFL-leading 29 regular-season sacks in the last two seasons.

"To get the quarterback, it becomes an addiction," the 6-foot-5, 280-pound defensive end explains. "It's like something you want so bad. You want to get there, and you're coming around the corner, and you'd like nothing more than just to wrap him up and pound him. Closing in on a quarterback, your eyes just get wide, and it's like the anticipation is just hard, hard to contain."

Carter doesn't try hard to contain it. There's far too much joy in single-handedly halting a play, forcing a punt and, sometimes, changing the course of the game.

"Once he sees that the quarterback still has the ball in his hand, it's like a steak," coach Dick Vermeil said. "He's going after it to take a bite out of it."

Twelve times in 1998, Carter experienced the rush of absolutely immobilizing a quarterback. Twelve sacks weren't enough, though. It wasn't enough to satiate him and wasn't enough to prompt an invitation to the Pro Bowl, though many argue he was more than deserving.

The rejection stung, his disappointment was strong, but Carter is a believer in the notion of blessings and curses.

"What I thought was a curse," says Carter, "not making it last year, was an inspiration to me to work harder, to do that much more. I said, 'Well, if you lead the league in sacks, they can't keep you out of the Pro Bowl, can they? . . . Let that be my goal this year. I want to lead the league in sacks. I want to let everyone know who can do it, who can play the run, who can play the pass, who can do it all and do it consistently.'"

His goal soundly met with 17 sacks, Carter is bound for the Pro Bowl.

"Kevin Carter's got a chance to be the best defensive end in the NFL, to dominate at the position for the next four or five years," said Charley Armey, Rams vice president of player personnel. "He's got quickness, strength, power, explosion, desire, intelligence. He's the total package."

One of Rams defensive line coach Carl Hairston's favorite training camp memories is of Carter coming off the ball so hard in practice that he knocked tight end Roland Williams' front four teeth out. Williams' braces were the only thing that prevented his teeth from falling to the turf.

"His teeth were swinging," Hairston recalled. "I asked (Carter) what triggered that. He said, 'Well, I just felt like doing it.' I said, 'Feel like doing it every time, because it's going to make people more afraid of you.

". . . When you look at Kevin, it's like he's been chiseled out of a block of ice. He plays with strength and finesse. That's intimidating for an offensive lineman, because you don't know exactly what Kevin's going to do."

1 2 3 4 5 6 7 8 9 10 11 12 13 14 15 16

GAME

11

NOV. 28, 1999
TRANS WORLD DOME
RAMS 43
SAINTS 12

WINNING IN LOW GEAR

◇

By Jim Thomas

The Rams didn't act like a beaten team — just one that had survived a narrow escape.

"We were lucky to get a win today," defensive tackle Ray Agnew said.

"We didn't play Ram football by a long shot," defensive tackle D'Marco Farr said.

"It sure as heck wasn't easy," coach Dick Vermeil said. "But at the end, you'd think it was a blowout."

Well, in defeating New Orleans 43-12 at the Trans World Dome, the Rams did:

■ Match their most lopsided victory margin of the season — 31 points.

■ Register the second-highest point total in a game since the 1990 season.

But it's a measure of how high the bar has been raised at Rams Park that such a victory would be accepted in measured tones.

"When you play as bad as we did and still score 43 points and hold them out of the end zone, that's big," Farr said. "That's just the mark of a good team, a winning team."

And make no mistake, the Rams are officially a winning team. At 9-2, the worst they can finish the regular season is 9-7. The franchise's nine-season losing streak is over. The city of St. Louis has its first winning NFL team since the 1984 Cardinals finished 9-7 under head coach Jim Hanifan.

But the Rams don't plan on stopping at No. 9. As safety Devin Bush put it: "We're in the driver's seat. Let's drive right on to Atlanta."

Atlanta, as you might have guessed, is the site of this season's Super Bowl.

With the outcome decided, Vermeil originally decided to take running back Marshall Faulk out on what would be the Rams' final drive. But the linemen told Vermeil they wanted to try to get 100 yards rushing for Faulk, who had 88 at the time. Vermeil relented. Faulk finished with 102 yards.

Tony Horne got the Rams off on a high note with his 64-yard return on the opening kickoff. That set up a Kurt Warner-to-Torry Holt touchdown pass less than a minute later. Horne was NFC special teams player of the week.

Torry Holt took in a 25-yard pass from Kurt Warner to give the Rams the lead after just 1 minute 2 seconds. Holt left his mark on the scoring column, breaking through for two TDs against the Saints after not scoring a touchdown since the second game of the season. "You have to stay patient. When they call your number, you step up and make the plays," he said.

	1ST	2ND	3RD	4TH	TOTAL
SAINTS	3	9	0	0	12
RAMS	7	8	7	21	43

SCORING SUMMARY

QTR	TEAM	PLAY		TIME
1st	**RAMS**	TD	Holt 25 yd. pass from Warner (Wilkins kick)	13:58
1st	**SAINTS**	FG	Brien 51 yds.	6:37
2nd	**SAINTS**	FG	Brien 42 yds.	14:56
2nd	**SAINTS**	FG	Brien 45 yds.	9:08
2nd	**RAMS**	TD	Faulk 1 yd. run (2 pt. conversion: Faulk run)	7:15
2nd	**SAINTS**	FG	Brien 35 yds.	:07
3rd	**RAMS**	TD	Faulk 6 yd. run (Wilkins kick)	3:08
4th	**RAMS**	TD	Holcombe 3 yd. run (Wilkins kick)	12:15
4th	**RAMS**	TD	Holt 20 yd. pass from Warner (Wilkins kick)	6:36
4th	**RAMS**	TD	Hodgins 1 yd. run (Wilkins kick)	1:14

Todd Lyght caught quarterback Billy Joe Hobert on the blind side with a second-quarter blitz, leading to an incompletion.

OFFENSE

SAINTS

PASSING	ATT	COMP	YDS	INT	TD
Billy Joe Hobert	41	23	254	2	0
Danny Wuerffel	6	2	19	0	0

RECEIVING	CATCHES	YDS	TD
Andre Hastings	9	113	
Cam Cleeland	5	62	
Eddie Kennison	5	33	
Lamar Smith	4	36	
Keith Poole	1	18	
Wilmont Perry	1	11	

RUSHING	RUSHES	YDS	TD
Lamar Smith	18	54	
Wilmont Perry	6	19	
Eddie Kennison	1	15	
Billy Joe Hobert	2	11	
Troy Davis	1	3	

RAMS

PASSING	ATT	COMP	YDS	INT	TD
Kurt Warner	27	15	213	0	2

RECEIVING	CATCHES	YDS	TD
Torry Holt	5	87	2
Isaac Bruce	5	81	
Az-Zahir Hakim	2	22	
Marshall Faulk	2	13	
Robert Holcombe	1	10	

RUSHING	RUSHES	YDS	TD
Marshall Faulk	18	102	2
Robert Holcombe	4	24	1
James Hodgins	3	3	1
Kurt Warner	2	0	

KEY TO THE GAME

The Saints had a chance to tie the game in the second half, but kicker Doug Brien missed a 24-yard field goal. The Rams then drove down the field as Kurt Warner completed five of five passes for 75 yards. A Marshall Faulk touchdown run capped the drive and gave the Rams a 22-12 lead.

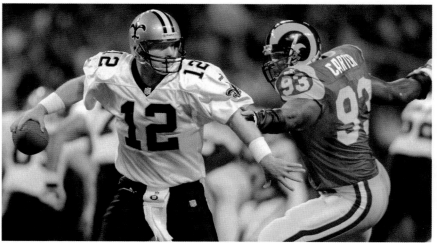

Billy Joe Hobert sparked a Saints offense that outgained the Rams in first-half yardage 202-78. By the second half, Kevin Carter & Co. had Hobert's number.

". . . they're good, let's face it. It wasn't like they just beat us.
They beat us in special teams. They dominated us.
And you know, that's better athletes that do that."

Saints coach **Mike Ditka**

Ron Carpenter (top) corralled the Saints' Dino Philyaw at the end of a 33-yard punt return.

Opponents for 60 minutes, the Rams and the Saints took part in a postgame prayer that has become an NFL ritual.

98

FINAL TAKE

BY BERNIE MIKLASZ

Watching the first half, the temptation was to head to a pay phone and place a call to the FBI. The Rams were missing. It could have been a kidnapping. Or maybe someone had taken them hostage. At minimum, this was a case of fraud. Who were these impostors?

This had to be Tony Banks at quarterback instead of Kurt Warner, because most of the passes nose-dived and crashed incomplete. That had to be the old offensive coaching staff running the offense in place of clever Mike Martz, because the Rams were wasting time and talent running Harry High School plays.

That had to be Robert Jones and Leslie O'Neal yawning and going through the motions on the Rams defense, because the visiting New Orleans Saints had everything but Al Hirt blowing the trumpet as they marched up and down the field.

Who let the Same Old Rams sneak back into the Dome, anyway?

From what I could tell, the plan was to have Warner stand and wait while the receivers ran slow-developing patterns that required approximately 17 minutes to finish. As Rams receivers ran out and crossed and curled, then ran back and crossed and curled again, I think I saw Hans Vonk of the St. Louis Symphony on the sideline conducting.

But in this remarkable season of change, the Rams turned back into themselves at halftime. They went out in the second half and gave Mike Ditka's team a severe case of rug burn, outscoring the Saints 28-0 in the final 30 minutes.

"Games like this build your confidence," D'Marco Farr said. "We were terrible but were still able to turn it around and get rolling and win big."

The upgrade in performance was encouraging. It shows that the Rams are adamant about quality; they will not allow themselves to coast through a mediocre game.

Charlie Clemons (56) earned the right to be an honorary Warner Brother with his fourth-quarter interception.

99

GAME
12
DEC. 5, 1999
ERICSSON STADIUM, CHARLOTTE, N.C.

RAMS	**34**
PANTHERS	**21**

HOW THE WEST WAS WON

◇

BY JIM THOMAS

It was a special moment for a maligned owner, Georgia Frontiere, and an oft-criticized front office headed by team President John Shaw.

Likewise for the five "LA" Rams: Isaac Bruce, D'Marco Farr, Todd Lyght, Keith Lyle and Jay Williams, who have experienced one losing season after another. And for the original "St. Louis" Ram: 1995 first-round draft pick Kevin Carter.

But the Rams wanted to let St. Louisans know that the 34-21 win over Carolina — and all it encompassed — was also for them.

"This is for the true-blue fans in St. Louis," Farr said. "The guys who have always been by our side and always cared about Rams football. ... This championship is theirs as much as it is ours."

The Rams got a career-high 351 yards passing by Kurt Warner, another 100-yard rushing day by Marshall Faulk, and two touchdown catches by Az-Zahir Hakim. Nursing a 24-21 lead in the fourth quarter, the Rams needed a 53-yard interception return for a TD by rookie Dre' Bly to put away Carolina and to make the Rams NFC West champions for the first time since 1985.

As a result, St. Louis gets a home playoff game for the first time in its pro football history, a period encompassing 28 seasons of the football Cardinals and five seasons of the Rams.

"The St. Louis fans stuck with us," Lyght said. "They never turned their backs on us. For us to bring it back home for them . . . it's our thanking the city of St. Louis."

Bill Bidwill's Cardinals made the playoffs in 1974, '75 and '82. But those were on the road and all first-round defeats.

"I know they were disappointed when they lost the St. Louis Cardinals," coach Dick Vermeil said. "But they've got a hell of a lot better organization in the St. Louis Rams.

"When they came here, they thought they could bring in a champion, and now they have one."

Dick Vermeil (center), owner Georgia Frontiere and Kurt Warner assembled in the closing seconds on the sideline in Charlotte, N.C., three prominent members of the Rams family brought together for a transcendent moment.

Marshall Faulk scooted away from the diving tackle attempt of Mike Minter in the third quarter of the Rams' division-clinching victory. Faulk finished with 118 yards rushing and 79 receiving but said: "There is a lot more that we want to fight for. It's like Stage 1 of the Tour de France."

	1ST	2ND	3RD	4TH	TOTAL
RAMS	14	7	0	13	34
PANTHERS	0	7	7	7	21

SCORING SUMMARY

QTR	TEAM	PLAY		TIME
1st	**RAMS**	TD	Williams 14 yd. pass from Warner (Wilkins kick)	10:12
1st	**RAMS**	TD	Hakim 48 yd. pass from Warner (Wilkins kick)	5:41
2nd	**RAMS**	TD	Hakim 49 yd. pass from Warner (Wilkins kick)	4:27
2nd	**PANTHERS**	TD	Walls 15 yd. pass from Beuerlein (Kasay kick)	:41
3rd	**PANTHERS**	TD	Hayes 36 yd. pass from Beuerlein (Kasay kick)	5:13
4th	**RAMS**	FG	Wilkins 44 yds.	14:56
4th	**PANTHERS**	TD	Jeffers 71 yd. pass from Beuerlein (Kasay kick)	14:31
4th	**RAMS**	TD	Bly 53 yd. interception return (Wilkins kick)	9:48
4th	**RAMS**	FG	Wilkins 29 yds.	3:39

KEY TO THE GAME

The Rams' big lead had been cut to 24-21, and momentum clearly was on the side of Carolina. Quarterback Steve Beuerlein's pass intended for Muhsin Muhammad went directly into the arms of Dre' Bly. Bly raced down the sideline 53 yards for a touchdown that knocked out the Panthers.

OFFENSE

RAMS

PASSING	ATT	COMP	YDS	INT	TD
Kurt Warner	31	22	351	2	3
Paul Justin	1	1	12	0	0

RECEIVING	CATCHES	YDS	TD
Isaac Bruce	6	111	
Marshall Faulk	6	79	
Az-Zahir Hakim	4	122	2
Ricky Proehl	4	31	
Roland Williams	2	16	1
Torry Holt	1	4	

RUSHING	RUSHES	YDS	TD
Marshall Faulk	22	118	
Robert Holcombe	8	10	
Kurt Warner	1	−1	
Az-Zahir Hakim	1	−3	

PANTHERS

PASSING	ATT	COMP	YDS	INT	TD
Steve Beuerlein	43	21	266	3	3

RECEIVING	CATCHES	YDS	TD
Patrick Jeffers	7	107	1
Muhsin Muhammad	4	46	
Wesley Walls	4	45	1
Tshimanga Biakabutuka	3	17	
Donald Hayes	1	36	1
Eric Metcalf	1	8	
William Floyd	1	7	

RUSHING	RUSHES	YDS	TD
Tshimanga Biakabutuka	11	42	
Steve Beuerlein	1	12	
Fred Lane	1	2	
William Floyd	2	1	
Michael Bates	1	-2	

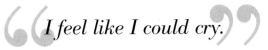

"I feel like I could cry."

Safety **Keith Lyle,** a longtime Ram, amid the dressing-room celebration after the team won the division title

Dick Vermeil (center) couldn't keep a lid on the enthusiasm as he, Kevin Carter (93) and D'Marco Farr walked off the field in Charlotte, N.C., wearing their "NFC West Champions" hats.

Dre' Bly (left) celebrated with London Fletcher after Bly's interception return broke the Panthers' comeback attempt in the fourth quarter.

FINAL TAKE

BY BERNIE MIKLASZ

It didn't take much effort for Rams coach Dick Vermeil to open his tear ducts. After defensive tackle Ray Agnew dropped to a knee to lead his teammates in prayer, Vermeil stood in the center of the locker room, voice cracking, and called his players champions.

Vermeil told them that they'd have a toast of champagne on the flight home. And then the coach reminded his team that they'd only just begun. Winning the NFC West title was the first major step in this incredible journey. But the Rams want to keep going. They want to keep marching right on into Atlanta for the Super Bowl.

"You know and I know that our goals go way beyond winning the division championship," a hoarse Vermeil told his players, who erupted in applause.

Vermeil turned the victory celebration over to Rams owner Georgia Frontiere. She removed her blue jacket to reveal a "St. Louis Rams, NFC Western Division Champions 1999" T-shirt.

The players started clapping again, and the equipment men continued handing out the special-issue championship caps and T-shirts. Wide receiver Isaac Bruce stuffed some souvenirs into his travel bag and headed off to a corner with a cell phone to call his mother and tell her the news: The Rams were the division champs.

"I'm so excited, so happy right now," Bruce said.

Bruce spoke for a lot of people. Mainly, the owners who moved the franchise to St. Louis, hoping for better days. And the patient, loyal football fans of St. Louis, who waited since 1975 to embrace a division winner. What started as a straight business deal has been consummated by a rich, emotional payoff.

Devin Bush high-fived the fans who waited for hours in cold, wet conditions at Lambert Field to welcome the team home. The Rams had touched down, but their following still was flying high.

105

HANDS OF STONE; SOLID AS A ROCK

———— ◇ ————

By Jim Thomas

Two weeks in a row during the 1999 season, linebacker Mike Jones put seven points on the board with long runs. Yet the debate rages on in the Rams' locker room.

Did Mike Jones really play running back in college?

The Rams have seen him drop too many interceptions in practice to take Jones' assertion at face value. Jones' muffs have become such legend at Rams Park that he was dubbed "Hands of Stone Jones."

Jones' touchdown theatrics have placed him in unfamiliar territory since joining the Rams in 1997 — the spotlight. The native of Kansas City usually is more in the background. He shows up, does his job, goes home. Week after week. Year after year.

"You appreciate Mike because you know you can count on him on an everyday basis," linebacker London Fletcher said.

"He's just solid as a rock," linebackers coach John Bunting said. "He's so happy that we're winning. He invests a lot of time in this community. He invests a lot of time in this team.

"When you try to do things right, and things don't go your way, you can lose sight of the big picture and take your eyes off the target. Mike Jones has never taken his eyes off the target."

Jones was among the first free agents brought in by newly hired coach Dick Vermeil after the 1996 season, but Bunting wasn't a big Jones-backer at the time.

"Quite frankly, I never thought he'd be the player he's become," Bunting said. "Never in my wildest dreams did I think he'd be able to play over the tight end like he has done."

In six seasons with the Raiders, Jones had always played weak-side linebacker — the side away from the tight end. In St. Louis, he always plays the left side. So whenever the tight end is on Jones' side, he must take him on.

Jones gradually turned a negative into a positive through hard work. He's now more than adequate at taking on tight ends.

"I don't think there's a linebacker in the league who covers as well as he does," Bunting said.

Jones didn't play linebacker at Mizzou. Despite the skepticism from his Rams teammates, Jones played running back his entire college career. It was Raiders owner Al Davis, after signing Jones as a rookie free agent in 1991, who decided to switch him to linebacker.

Learning the nuances of the position has been a gradual process.

"It's still a process to this day," Jones said. "One of my coaches was saying it took three to four years to learn how to play linebacker in the NFL, even if you played it in college. I still make some mistakes."

But he has become a good, all-around linebacker. His teammates gave Jones the 1999 Spirit of the Game Award, which goes to the player who best exemplifies work ethic and committment to his teammates.

SWEEPING UP IN THE WEST

◇

BY JIM THOMAS

Take it from Todd Lyght: The view from the NFC West summit is breathtaking.

"To come from the cellar to sitting with this penthouse view is a beautiful thing for us," Lyght said.

The Rams completed the most dramatic worst-to-first turnaround in NFL history, defeating the New Orleans Saints 30-14 in the Superdome.

After going 0-8 in the NFC West a year ago, the Rams finished division play with an 8-0 record. They thus became the only NFL team ever to go from winless to unbeaten in division play from one season to the next.

"That's a tribute to our ownership, our management, my coaching staff and the personnel department," coach Dick Vermeil said. "When you do that, no one does it by himself. No one running back, no one quarterback, no one head coach, no one assistant. Your whole organization has to be doing things right."

The Rams didn't just sweep the NFC West, they blew it away.

The average score against division foes: 35-13. The narrowest margin of victory: 13 points.

As strange as it might sound for a team that piled up a season-high 492 yards in offense, it was only a workmanlike performance. Had the Rams been on their game, they would have hung up half a hundred on the Saints.

"We started slow both offensively and defensively," Lyght said. "We don't want to get into the habit of that. But sometimes it can be tough to get up for games. The stadium really wasn't that filled."

Half-filled would be more like it. Didn't matter to Marshall Faulk, though. He was in a league of his own, with 154 yards rushing and 210 total yards. "There were some plays out there today that just made me laugh," quarterback Kurt Warner said, "because the guy's incredibly talented."

Dexter McCleon leaped to bat away a potential touchdown pass to Eddie Kennison in the second quarter. The Rams kept their ex-teammate under control, limiting Kennison to just 19 yards on two receptions.

Jay Williams reeled in Billy Joe Tolliver for a 13-yard loss, one of two sacks Williams had in New Orleans.

OFFENSE

RAMS

PASSING	ATT	COMP	YDS	INT	TD
Kurt Warner	31	21	346	1	2

RECEIVING	CATCHES	YDS	TD
Torry Holt	6	113	
Marshall Faulk	5	56	1
Isaac Bruce	4	102	
Roland Williams	2	26	
Ricky Proehl	2	23	
Az-Zahir Hakim	1	25	
Robert Holcombe	1	1	1

RUSHING	RUSHES	YDS	TD
Marshall Faulk	29	154	1
Kurt Warner	2	4	
Paul Justin	2	-2	
Robert Holcombe	1	0	

SAINTS

PASSING	ATT	COMP	YDS	INT	TD
Billy Joe Tolliver	28	12	188	3	1

RECEIVING	CATCHES	YDS	TD
Keith Poole	3	83	
Andre Hastings	2	45	
Eddie Kennison	2	19	
Lamar Smith	2	15	
Troy Davis	1	20	
Wilmont Perry	1	4	
Cam Cleeland	1	2	1

RUSHING	RUSHES	YDS	TD
Wilmont Perry	14	54	
Billy Joe Tolliver	1	6	
Andre Hastings	1	4	
Troy Davis	1	2	
Dino Philyaw	1	0	

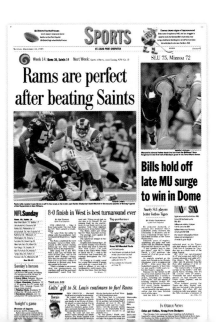

	1ST	2ND	3RD	4TH	TOTAL
RAMS	7	17	3	3	30
SAINTS	6	8	0	0	14

SCORING SUMMARY

QTR	TEAM	PLAY	TIME
1st	**SAINTS**	FG	Brien 29 yds. 10:41
1st	**RAMS**	TD	Holcombe 1 yd. pass from Warner (Wilkins kick) ..5:39
1st	**SAINTS**	FG	Brien 26 yds. 1:29
2nd	**SAINTS**	TD	Cleeland 2 yd. pass from Tolliver (2 pt. conversion: Kennison pass from Tolliver) 9:09
2nd	**RAMS**	FG	Wilkins 40 yds. 7:24
2nd	**RAMS**	TD	Faulk 4 yd. run (Wilkins kick) 3:28
2nd	**RAMS**	TD	Faulk 30 yd. pass from Warner (Wilkins kick) .... :51
3rd	**RAMS**	FG	Wilkins 30 yds. 5:40
4th	**RAMS**	FG	Wilkins 38 yds. 2:29

KEY TO THE GAME

Interceptions late in the first half rocked the Saints. With New Orleans leading 14-10, Todd Lyght picked off a Billy Joe Tolliver pass and returned it to the Rams 41, setting up a six-play, 59-yard TD drive. And then, Dexter McCleon intercepted another pass and put the Rams in Saints territory at the 47. Five plays later, Marshall Faulk was in the end zone on a 30-yard pass from Kurt Warner.

Billy Joe Tolliver spent much of the afternoon inspecting the carpet at the Superdome. The Saints quarterback was sacked six times for 44 yards in losses.

Marshall Faulk's 210 yards of total offense helped the Rams to a Sunday afternoon cruise in New Orleans. "We felt like we could have scored 50 had we taken advantage of all the situations," Kurt Warner said.

Dexter McCleon's second-quarter interception helped put the Rams in position for the scoring drive that would give them a 24-14 lead and put them in control at halftime.

FINAL TAKE

BY BERNIE MIKLASZ

Marshall Faulk had an eventful homecoming.

He visited with his mom, Cecile. He threw a party for friends and family at the House of Blues. He dined on some shrimp Creole at K-Paul's. He handed out 75 tickets for the game, creating a personal cheering section at the Louisiana Superdome.

Then, he went out and ran about 5 miles through the Saints defense. The Rams had to overcome boredom to dispose of the Saints, and this victory had Faulk's shoeprints all over it.

Thank you, Indianapolis, for sending Faulk to the Rams for two draft picks. The Rams did not even have to trade a warm body for Faulk. They get the league's best all-around running back for a couple of sheets of NFL paper-work?

As St. Louis trades go, this ranks up there with getting Lou Brock for Ernie Broglio, Mark McGwire for three young pitchers, and Brett Hull for Rob Ramage and Rick Wamsley. This was the best trade made by Rams president John Shaw since he swapped the empty seats in Anaheim for a full house in St. Louis.

In the Rams' first four seasons in St. Louis, they had only six 100-yard games by a back. Faulk had seven in the first 13 games. Make sure to send the Colts an extra holiday fruitcake this month.

Except for their unwillingness to give Faulk the kind of salary he deserved, there is no clear reason why the Colts donated him to the Rams' charitable foundation. Faulk is 26, not 36. There's ample tread on those tires.

"You get him out in the open, and there's not one man that's going to tackle him," tackle Fred Miller said. "He's going to make you look real bad, and you're going to be on his highlight video."

The highlight video alone is worth two draft choices.

Dick Vermeil, headed for the summit, tried to extend encouragement to beleaguered colleague Mike Ditka (right) before the game. Vermeil would be selected as NFL coach of the year. Ditka was fired after the Saints' 3-13 season.

THE SPIRIT OF ST. LOUIS

◇

BY JIM THOMAS

In front of a record St. Louis football crowd, the Rams became a record St. Louis football team.

Their 31-10 thrashing of the New York Giants made them the winningest team in the history of St. Louis pro football. Back in the days of the 14-game schedule, the St. Louis Cardinals went 11-3 in 1975.

Nearly a quarter of a century later, the St. Louis Rams are 12-2 — and counting.

"For what the fans have done for us, to give them 12 wins is great," linebacker Mike Jones said.

The fans were there 66,065 strong at the Trans World Dome. Not only did the Rams present them with a piece of local football history, but they also gave them home-field advantage for the NFC playoffs.

"St. Louis deserves something like this," coach Dick Vermeil said. "There are a lot of nice people here. I went to the grocery store yesterday, and I could not believe the reaction I got. And all I did was get some apple cider."

What, no Warner's Crunch Time cereal? Vermeil laughed. "These people are into it, and I think now they feel the Rams are really 'St. Louis' Rams," he said.

As the top seed in the NFC, the Rams get a first-round playoff bye.

"To have that bye will be very meaningful," Vermeil said. "Not only for the players but my coaches. We all run out of gas, too."

Adding fuel to their fire were pregame comments by the Giants. OK, it was hardly "remember the Alamo" material, but it got the Rams' attention. A copy of the article was circulated in the Rams' locker room by coaches.

"It got a whole bunch of people mad in here," Jones said.

By game's end, the Rams had dropped five passes and had lost a fumble in the red zone. So, it was far from their crispest offensive performance. Still, they gained 412 yards ... and won by 21 points.

Taje Allen (20) batted away a fourth-quarter pass intended for the Giants' Joe Jurevicius. The Rams kept the Giants offense under wraps until a meaningless touchdown in the last five minutes.

Mike Jones went into Dance Fever mode as he prepared to do a defensive rendition of the time-honored Bob & Weave after a 22-yard, fourth-quarter interception return for a touchdown. Dexter McCleon (21), Kevin Carter (93) and Nate Hobgood-Chittick also high-stepped it on a day in which the defense (two TDs) boogied as much as the offense.

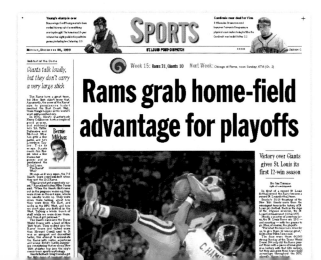

UPON FURTHER REVIEW ...

1) **Az-Zahir Hakim** went high to snare a Kurt Warner pass in the back of the end zone. But not so fast ...

2) Back judge **Jack Vaughan** signaled that Hakim was beyond the end line as Isaac Bruce (80) and Hakim lobbied for a TD ...

3) And **Torry Holt** proved to be one step ahead of the officials, who eventually ruled that Hakim was shoved out of bounds and that it was a touchdown.

Marshall Faulk had the Giants' undivided attention as he split their defense for a 27-yard run in the first quarter. Faulk had 165 yards of total offense, including 97 receiving. That left him at 2,065 yards from scrimmage through 14 games.

	1ST	2ND	3RD	4TH	TOTAL
GIANTS	0	0	3	7	10
RAMS	3	7	7	14	31

SCORING SUMMARY

QTR	TEAM	PLAY	TIME
1st	**RAMS**	FG	Wilkins 47 yds. 3:24
2nd	**RAMS**	TD	Hakim 3 yd. pass from Warner (Wilkins kick) 13:31
3rd	**GIANTS**	FG	Blanchard 23 yds. 10:08
3rd	**RAMS**	TD	Bush 45 yd. interception return (Wilkins kick) 5:25
4th	**RAMS**	TD	Hakim 65 yd. pass from Warner (Wilkins kick) ...13:58
4th	**RAMS**	TD	M. Jones 22 yd. interception return (Wilkins kick).7:10
4th	**GIANTS**	TD	Hilliard 7 yd. pass from Collins (Blanchard kick)...4:48

Kevin Carter, who had one sack, took a breather during a first half in which the Rams controlled play but could score only 10 points.

OFFENSE

GIANTS

PASSING	ATT	COMP	YDS	INT	TD
Kerry Collins	37	21	273	2	1

RECEIVING	CATCHES	YDS	TD
Amani Toomer	9	162	
Ike Hilliard	5	51	1
Tiki Barber	3	43	
Pete Mitchell	2	16	
Greg Comella	2	1	

RUSHING	RUSHES	YDS	TD
Joe Montgomery	12	41	
Tiki Barber	5	33	
Kerry Collins	1	-1	
Ike Hilliard	1	-6	

RAMS

PASSING	ATT	COMP	YDS	INT	TD
Kurt Warner	32	18	319	0	2

RECEIVING	CATCHES	YDS	TD
Marshall Faulk	6	97	
Torry Holt	5	70	
Az-Zahir Hakim	3	79	2
Isaac Bruce	2	39	
Ricky Proehl	1	30	
Roland Williams	1	4	

RUSHING	RUSHES	YDS	TD
Marshall Faulk	16	68	
Robert Holcombe	8	20	
Kurt Warner	2	10	
James Hodgins	1	2	

<u>KEY TO THE GAME</u>

Devin Bush, a starter at free safety after Keith Lyle was injured, intercepted an overthrown ball and returned it 45 yards for a touchdown. It gave the Rams a 17-3 lead in the third quarter.

> *"Give them credit. They did what they had to do.*
> *I was impressed with their offense."*

Giants free safety **Percy Ellsworth**

Devin Bush tumbled into the end zone with a 45-yard, third-quarter interception return that signaled the beginning of the end for the Giants.

FINAL TAKE

BY BERNIE MIKLASZ

The Rams have a great team, but New York didn't know that. Apparently, the news of the Rams' rise to prominence hadn't reached the East Coast. Well, these things happen in the world's most self-absorbed city.

In NYC, Giants quarterback Kerry Collins can have a couple of good games, and suddenly he's Y.A. Tittle. Defensive end Michael Strahan gets a few sacks, and he's Lawrence Taylor. This is where Giants coach Jim Fassel wins a few December games and is proclaimed the Dalai Lama.

The Rams? Who?

The Giants came into the Trans World Dome with a load of New York trash. They walked into the Rams' house and talked more than Howard Cosell used to. It was an arrogant and dimwitted tactic, this attempt to intimidate the Rams with verbs, adjectives and nouns. But it's hardly surprising considering that so many New York athletes buy into the city's comic-book sports mythology.

The Rams did a Travis Bickle on the Giants. First, they responded with the standard, "Are you talking to me?" And then, the Rams whacked the Giants 31-10 to secure home-field advantage throughout the NFC playoffs.

By the end of the game, the Giants had lost their vocal cords. The Giants made too many mistakes. Their first was not realizing that the Rams are hooked on phonics. There is no shortage of linguists in the Rams locker room. The Rams are the Winston Churchill of trash talk.

The Giants' weak physical follow-up to the brave dialogue disgusted Rams cornerback Todd Lyght, who was expecting a skirmish. Instead, Lyght got some ballroom dancing lessons.

"I can't believe these people would put themselves out there like that," Lyght said. "With all that tough talk and then to come in here and make no plays and be so delicate, what are they thinking?"

Kurt Warner and his wife, Brenda, per their custom, seal victory with a kiss.

THE MIRACLE ON I-70

——— ◇ ———

BY BERNIE MIKLASZ

His car was out of control after blowing the rear left tire, skidding away from eastbound Interstate 70, headed toward the gully, about to roll over, driver-side first.

By now, you probably have heard the play-by-play of that scene Dec. 7. About how Rams wide receiver Isaac Bruce, who makes a living catching footballs with his hands, took those precious hands off the steering wheel, raised them into the air and shouted "Jesus!" for protection.

The Mercedes-Benz flipped twice before crash-landing upright.

Mashed, but standing. Hey, the bump-and-run never could stop Isaac Bruce.

And Bruce, who had escaped death and serious injury, thought of three things.

First, the health of his girlfriend, who was seated on the passenger side. She was fine, with a small cut on her forehead.

Next, his condition. Bruce stretched his arms and flexed his legs. No problem.

And the third thing that came into his mind was pound cake.

Pound cake?

"I didn't even think about dying," Bruce said. "It never hit my mind that, 'I could have died here.' Honestly, I was thinking about getting (his girlfriend) out of the car and how I was going to get my pound cake. I was planning to pick it up that night."

A star athlete walks away from an accident that easily could have left him paralyzed, twisted like a pretzel or in a casket. But he doesn't even chip a tooth, get a bump on his head or rip his trousers.

A Rams employee who saw the wrecked car would recount the scene and exhale, shake his head and whisper that it's a miracle to have Isaac Bruce still among us. And that maybe this is another sign that the Rams really are a team of destiny in 1999.

But in the immediate moments after death took a pass and floated over that Mercedes-Benz and moved on down the highway, Isaac Bruce was thinking about ... pound cake?

"It's pound cake that I buy from this lady in St. Louis," Bruce said. "I love pound cake. Every night, I have a slice of pound cake with vanilla ice cream. It's what I eat. I was out of pound cake, and I wanted to get that pound cake. And I had the accident, and I knew I couldn't pick up my pound cake."

When Bruce was asked if he had feared dying as the car tumbled over, he responded:

"I knew what the outcome would be once I spoke the name of Jesus. Once I got that out of my mouth, I wasn't afraid. I knew I was covered by the blood of Jesus."

The day after the accident, Bruce read Psalm 91, his favorite, which says, in part:

"Because he loves me," says the Lord, "I will rescue him; I will protect him, for he acknowledges my name. He will call upon me and I will answer him; I will be with him in trouble, I will deliver him ..."

When your Christian faith is so strong, Isaac was saying, you have no reason to fear death. You shout "Jesus" and walk away from a mangled car. And the only thing you worry about is pound cake. Now that's faith.

Isaac finally picked up his new pound cake three nights later.

He says it never tasted better.

123456789101112131415 16

DEC. 26, 1999
TRANS WORLD DOME

GAME
15

RAMS 34
BEARS 12

FAULK BY LAND, FAULK BY AIR

—— ◇ ——

BY JIM THOMAS

The best tackle of the day was made by gray-haired umpire Jim Quirk, who was so determined to break up a scuffle that he took down Rams tight end Jeff Robinson.

The catch of the day was made by 263-pound defensive end Grant Wistrom, on an interception.

But the best indication that things were a tad goofy in the Rams' 34-12 victory over Chicago at the Trans World Dome?

That would be the sight of Chicago trying to cover Marshall Faulk out of the backfield with . . . a linebacker! Over and over again.

It was almost as if the Bears' defensive coaches were out Christmas shopping last week whenever Faulk was shown on game film running pass patterns.

The Rams did everything but send a note to the Bears sideline with the message: "Pssst. You might want to cover No. 28."

"That linebacker, he needed help," Rams cornerback Todd Lyght said, referring to the Bears' Barry Minter. "We kept trying to tell them, 'Hey, you need to get some help.' We'll take that matchup all the time."

The Rams took it all right. Twelve times for 204 reception yards for Faulk.

"I used to think if I could have any back, I would want Barry Sanders," Rams defensive tackle Ray Agnew said. "My opinion has changed. I'll take Marshall Faulk."

Faulk's big receiving day made him only the second player in NFL history to record 1,000 yards receiving and 1,000 yards rushing in the same season. Roger Craig did it in 1985 for San Francisco.

It was just one of many milestones for the Rams. But the most important was the victory. The triumph gave the Rams a 13-2 record, making the '99 squad the winningest team in the 62-year history of the Cleveland/Los Angeles/St. Louis Rams.

---

124 **Jeff Robinson** (45) found himself on the receiving end of one of the day's best takedowns, by umpire Jim Quirk, who did what the Bears had difficulty doing to Rams ballcarriers. Quirk was breaking up an altercation, and Robinson was ejected.

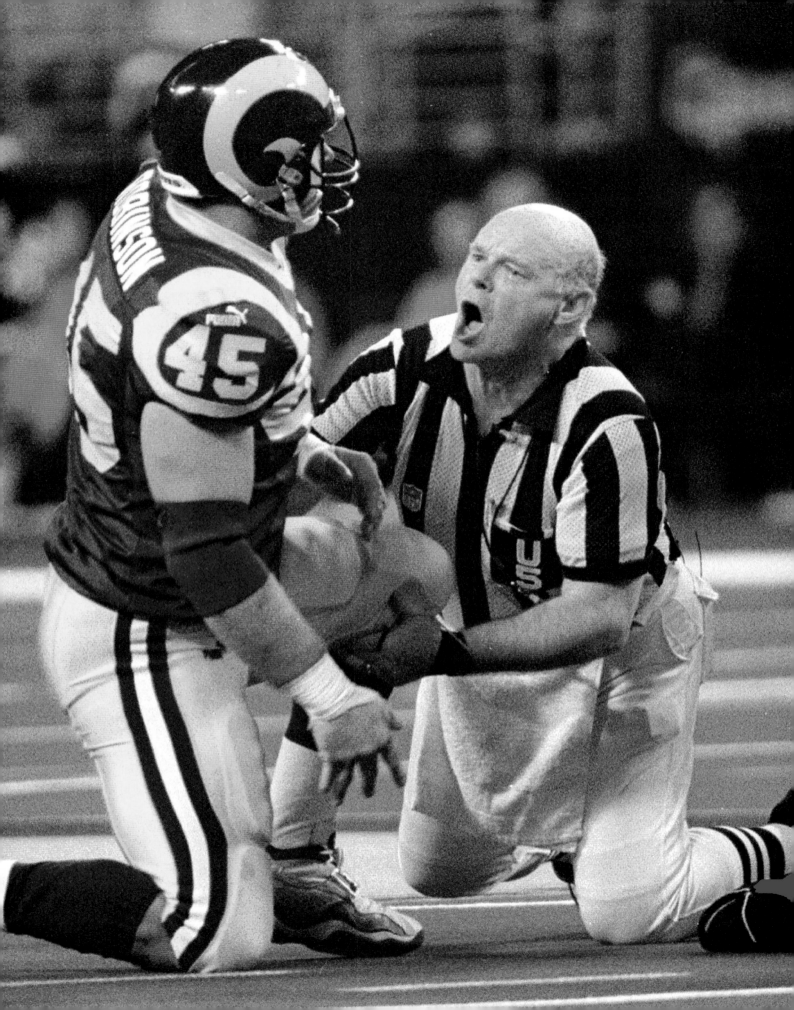

Ricky Proehl
kept the Rams
Express on track
with a 13-yard
reception in the
third quarter.

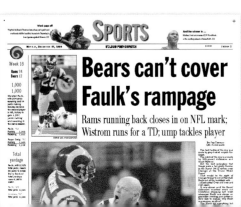

Marshall Faulk throttled down after motoring past the Bears for a 48-yard touchdown on a screen pass in the second quarter. With 12 catches for 204 yards, Faulk became only the second player in NFL history to record 1,000 yards in receptions and 1,000 yards rushing in the same season. Faulk was selected as NFC offensive player of the week for the second time in the '99 season. Going into the final week, Faulk was just 35 yards short of Barry Sanders' league record of 2,358 yards from scrimmage.

	1ST	2ND	3RD	4TH	TOTAL
BEARS	0	0	6	6	12
RAMS	0	17	14	3	34

SCORING SUMMARY

QTR	TEAM	PLAY		TIME
2nd	**RAMS**	TD	Faulk 48 yd. pass from Warner (Wilkins kick)	8:36
2nd	**RAMS**	TD	Williams 2 yd. pass from Warner (Wilkins kick)	2:11
2nd	**RAMS**	FG	Wilkins 38 yds.	:44
3rd	**RAMS**	TD	Bruce 4 yd. pass from Warner (Wilkins kick)	9:59
3rd	**RAMS**	TD	Wistrom 40 yd. interception return (Wilkins kick)	8:08
3rd	**BEARS**	TD	Engram 8 yd. pass from Matthews (kick missed)	3:00
4th	**BEARS**	TD	Engram 4 yd. pass from Matthews (2 pt. failed)	11:18
4th	**RAMS**	FG	Wilkins 28 yds.	5:05

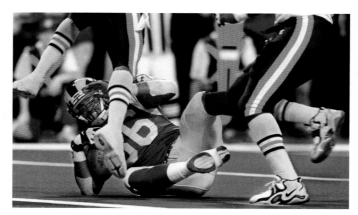

Roland Williams hauled in a second-quarter pass from Kurt Warner.

OFFENSE

BEARS

PASSING	ATT	COMP	YDS	INT	TD
Shane Matthews	39	23	266	1	2
Cade McNown	16	9	125	1	0

RECEIVING	CATCHES	YDS	TD
Bobby Engram	13	143	2
Marcus Robinson	6	93	
James Allen	5	63	
Ryan Wetnight	4	26	
John Allred	2	34	
Alonzo Mayes	1	24	
Marty Booker	1	8	

RUSHING	RUSHES	YDS	TD
James Allen	6	30	
Curtis Enis	7	21	
Cade McNown	3	18	
Shane Matthews	1	0	

RAMS

PASSING	ATT	COMP	YDS	INT	TD
Kurt Warner	35	24	334	1	3
Paul Justin	7	3	27	0	0

RECEIVING	CATCHES	YDS	TD
Marshall Faulk	12	204	1
Isaac Bruce	4	45	1
Torry Holt	3	33	
Az-Zahir Hakim	2	40	
Ricky Proehl	2	19	
Roland Williams	2	4	1
Robert Holcombe	1	10	
Jeff Robinson	1	6	

RUSHING	RUSHES	YDS	TD
Marshall Faulk	10	54	
Robert Holcombe	3	24	
Justin Watson	11	23	
Isaac Bruce	2	11	
Paul Justin	1	3	

KEY TO THE GAME

Marshall Faulk's 48-yard touchdown reception got the offense rolling after a scoreless first quarter. It was on a screen pass, something that had been the Rams' bread and butter all season. "It was just set up pretty," Faulk said. "Tommy Nutten was out in front, I got the first two blocks and it was up to me."

Trust me now, this is a talented football team.
They don't have home-field (playoff) advantage by accident.

Bears defensive coordinator **Greg Blache**

Roland Williams' second-quarter touchdown catch sent the Ram tote board to even higher totals. The Rams finished the day with a team-record 495 points, besting the 466-point total scored by the 1950 Rams.

1 2 3 4 5 6 7 8 9 10 11 12 13 14 15 16

DEC. 26, 1999
TRANS WORLD DOME
GAME
15

RAMS 34
BEARS 12

FINAL TAKE

BY BERNIE MIKLASZ

It was Christmas weekend, a perfect time for the Rams to take a winter's nap. The Rams already had put the pretty paper, the ribbon and the bows on the regular season by clinching home-field advantage in the NFC playoffs.

But instead of being fat and happy and unable to budge from their easy chairs, the Rams showed up with a ravenous, greedy appetite for more team success, more personal glory, more holiday cheer.

Watching the Rams attack a "meaningless" game like this made you wonder: Don't these guys ever get tired? Do they ever play at anything less than warp speed? Where's the complacency that should have settled in by now?

The game's final play was telling. With the Rams leading 34-12, the Bears completed a 26-yard pass to tight end John Allred, who caught the ball near the goal line. Allred tried to barge in, but several Rams defenders ganged up and wouldn't give an inch. Allred kept churning his legs; the Rams defensive backs swarmed and held him up at the 2-yard line until the final whistle sounded.

A touchdown would mean little in that situation. But to the Rams defense, keeping Allred out of the end zone meant everything.

"I think they're disciplined to play," coach Dick Vermeil said. "They like to play. They like each other. They care about each other. They care about their coaches. They care about their organization. They care about their city."

That's one of the most impressive qualities about the Rams: They don't take days off. They don't even take plays off. The Rams don't call in sick. Except for one bad half at Tennessee and one meek defensive series at Detroit, the Rams haven't wavered. They've been the league's most consistent team.

And that's why they're the best team.

Dre' Bly (left) moved in to push the Bears' Marcus Robinson out of bounds after a second-quarter reception.

1234567891011121314
JAN. 2, 2000
VETERANS STADIUM, PHILADELPHIA
GAME **16**
EAGLES 38
RAMS 31

PLEASE JUST STAY HEALTHY

———— ◇ ————

BY JIM THOMAS

The Rams committed a month's worth of turnovers. Dropped more than their normal share of passes.

And may have missed as many tackles as in their previous 15 games combined.

Leaving a day early from St. Louis because of league-mandated Y2K concerns, the Rams brought an extra set of clothes. But they forgot to pack their intensity for what became a 38-31 loss to Philadelphia.

With their seven-game winning streak over and a 13-3 regular-season record, the Rams should take two things from this game:

■ The mere act of stepping on the field won't be enough to ensure victory in the playoffs. The Rams are not invincible.

■ If they commit seven turnovers and are minus 5 in giveaways-takeaways — as was the case against the Eagles — they will make an early exit in the playoffs.

But you know what? It just doesn't matter. When the Rams open the playoffs at the Trans World Dome, no one will be thinking about the events of Jan. 2 at Veterans Stadium.

"This was like a preseason game," wide receiver Isaac Bruce said. "It really didn't mean anything. We proved last week that we could play for nothing when we played against Chicago."

But the Rams achieved one of their primary goals of the trip: to keep everyone injury free.

And they reached a number of team and individual milestones.

Marshall Faulk finished with 2,429 total yards, breaking Barry Sanders' NFL record.

Kurt Warner became just the second player in NFL history to throw as many as 40 touchdown passes (41) in a season.

With one sack, **Kevin Carter** finished as the NFL's sack champion with 17.

But just like the final score, none of that matters anymore. As Bruce said, "It's time for the playoffs now."

Joe Germaine gained some valuable — and at times painful — experience at quarterback in relief of Kurt Warner. He was nine of 16 for 136 yards passing, but his fourth-quarter interception that was returned for a touchdown proved to be the difference.

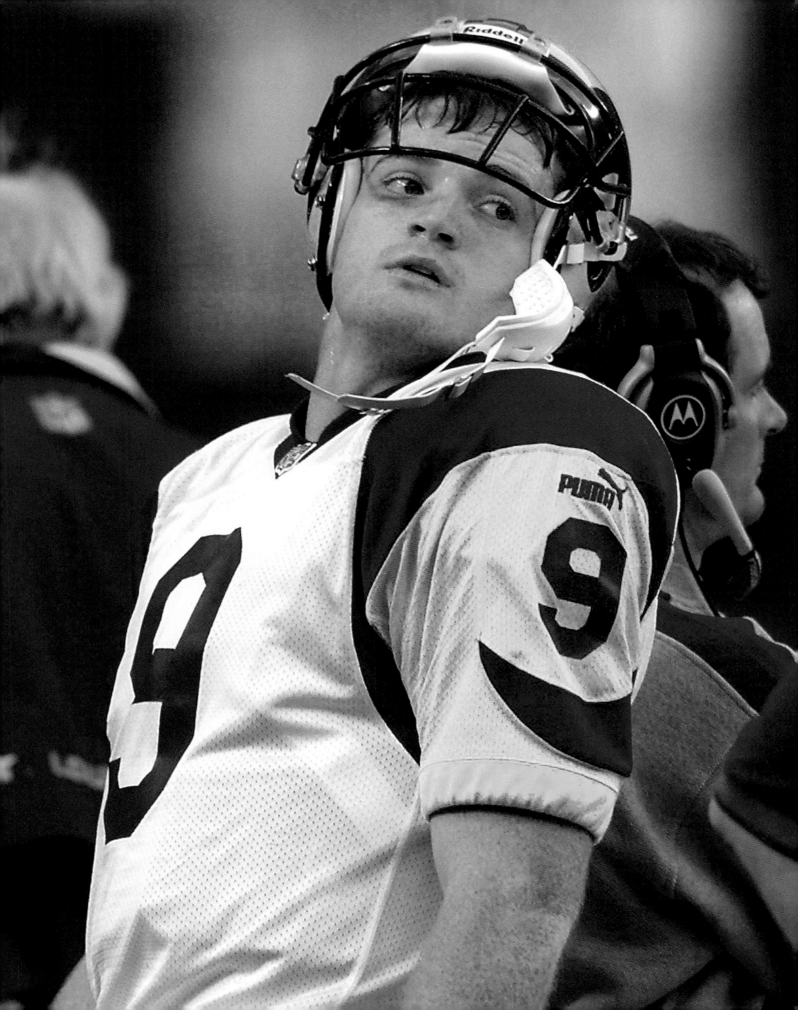

Robert Holcombe (right) lost the football on this second-quarter hit, but the play had been blown dead. On seven other occasions, however, the Rams proved to be generous guests, giving their hosts three fumbles and four interceptions.

	1ST	2ND	3RD	4TH	TOTAL
RAMS	7	10	7	7	31
EAGLES	3	14	7	14	38

SCORING SUMMARY

QTR	TEAM	PLAY		TIME
1st	**RAMS**	TD	Faulk 8 yd. pass from Warner (Wilkins kick)	9:42
1st	**EAGLES**	FG	Akers 46 yds.	7:27
2nd	**RAMS**	TD	Faulk 1 yd. run (Wilkins kick)	11:57
2nd	**EAGLES**	TD	Small 63 yd. pass from McNabb (Johnson kick)	10:14
2nd	**RAMS**	FG	Wilkins 47 yds.	6:20
2nd	**EAGLES**	TD	Staley 3 yd. pass from McNabb (Johnson kick)	:32
3rd	**EAGLES**	TD	Mamula 41 yd. interception return (Johnson kick)	12:15
3rd	**RAMS**	TD	Holt 15 yd. pass from Warner (Wilkins kick)	9:22
4th	**EAGLES**	TD	Lewis 5 yd. pass from McNabb (Johnson kick)	10:55
4th	**EAGLES**	TD	Harris 17 yd. interception return (Johnson kick)	1:16
4th	**RAMS**	TD	Holt 63 yd. pass from Germaine (Wilkins kick)	:59

Torry Holt knelt as he caught Kurt Warner's final pass of the regular season, a 15-yard TD reception in the third quarter. Warner joined Dan Marino as the only men in NFL history to throw for 40 or more touchdown passes in a season.

OFFENSE

EAGLES

PASSING	ATT	COMP	YDS	INT	TD
Donovan McNabb	32	15	179	2	3

RECEIVING	CATCHES	YDS	TD
Torrance Small	6	98	1
Na Brown	3	26	
Chad Lewis	2	26	1
Duce Staley	2	14	1
Cecil Martin	1	9	
Luther Broughton	1	6	

RUSHING	RUSHES	YDS	TD
Duce Staley	18	44	
Donovan McNabb	5	7	

RAMS

PASSING	ATT	COMP	YDS	INT	TD
Kurt Warner	24	12	141	2	2
Joe Germaine	16	9	136	2	1

RECEIVING	CATCHES	YDS	TD
Torry Holt	5	122	2
Ricky Proehl	5	61	
Marshall Faulk	3	27	1
Robert Holcombe	2	20	
Az-Zahir Hakim	2	16	
James Hodgins	2	11	
Ernie Conwell	1	11	
Roland Williams	1	9	

RUSHING	RUSHES	YDS	TD
Robert Holcombe	15	86	
Marshall Faulk	6	79	1
Az-Zahir Hakim	1	31	
Justin Watson	3	3	
Joe Germaine	1	2	

ST. LOUIS POST-DISPATCH

SPORTS

Week 17

Eagles 38
Rams 31

Records
WRAPUP

Marshall Faulk
▸ Finished with
166 yards to
give him
2,429 yards
from scrimmage,
passing Barry
Sanders' mark of
2,358 yards

Kurt Warner
▸ Became second
player in history
to throw 40 TD
passes. Dan
Marino threw for
48 TDs ('84) and
44 TDs ('86).
▸ Finished with
4,353 yards,
a new Rams
record.

Kevin Carter
▸ Picked up his
17th sack for

Eagles make the Rams pay for outbreak of turnovers

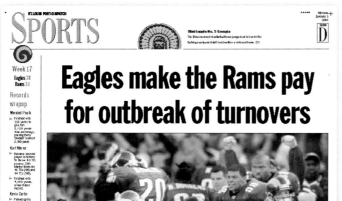

KEY TO THE GAME

The Rams accomplished their biggest objectives: avoiding injuries, picking up a few personal milestones and keeping the starters sharp. After a so-so first half, Kurt Warner showed his MVP form in leading the Rams on a six-play, 67-yard drive in the third quarter. His 15-yard pass to Torry Holt capped the drive and gave Warner 41 touchdown passes for the season.

*Right now, I'm thinking more about January
and what I want to accomplish there. Not what I've accomplished so far.*

Kurt Warner

Marshall Faulk high-stepped into the end zone on a 1-yard TD run in the second quarter just before being yanked from the game to guard against injury. "You take Marshall Faulk out of the ballgame, you're going into second gear," coach Dick Vermeil said. Faulk finished his record-breaking run, amassing 2,429 yards from scrimmage to better Barry Sanders' mark.

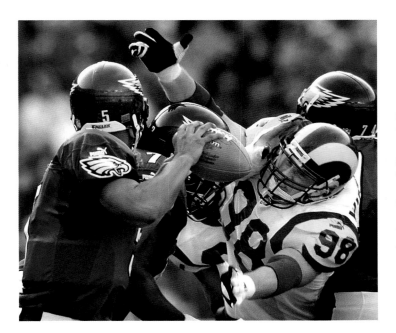

Grant Wistrom pressured the Eagles' Donovan McNabb, who was able to get off the pass in the second quarter. The Rams did manage to tack on three sacks to finish with a team-record 57, which tied for the NFL lead with Jacksonville.

1234567891011121314

JAN. 2, 2000
VETERANS STADIUM, PHILADELPHIA

GAME
16

EAGLES 38
RAMS 31

FINAL TAKE

BY BERNIE MIKLASZ

The last time a St. Louis sports team played at Veterans Stadium, Cardinals center fielder J.D. Drew had to dodge batteries thrown at him by irate Phillies fans. Drew escaped from Philly with his body in one piece.

The Rams had to maneuver through a similar challenge as they closed the NFL regular season: Get out of this cesspool of a stadium in good health.

Mission accomplished. Those of you who were holding your breath in fear of playoff-altering injuries may exhale now. Their egos were a little tender, but no stretchers, crutches or ambulances were needed to transport the Rams back to St. Louis.

Yes, it was a minor indignity for the Rams' junior varsity to lose to the Eagles. It was ugly watching the Rams turn the ball over seven times. And it was annoying to see the 5-11 Eagles carrying on as if they had actually accomplished something more meaningful than outlasting the St. Louis scrubs.

But this was a healthy loss. Given a choice, the Rams would rather lose to the Eagles than win this game and lose Marshall Faulk, Kurt Warner, Isaac Bruce, Kevin Carter, Orlando Pace or any other notable starting player.

Warner played long enough to become the second NFL quarterback to strike for 40 TD passes in a season. But the best thing about Warner's game? He survived it. So did all the Rams. Their blase effort can be excused. They had one eye on the stadium exit, one eye on the playoffs.

"We're going to be ready come playoff time," Warner said.

Nothing else matters now. The Rams are beginning their quest for the Super Bowl, and all of their body parts are working. The Rams lost, but the team doctors didn't pick up any new patients. That's a winner.

Dick Vermeil's Philly homecoming was a downer for the second year in a row. But with the Rams going home to camp out for the playoffs, this loss didn't sting as much.

135

HE'LL FIND AN EDGE ANY WAY HE CAN

◇

BY VAHE GREGORIAN

Rams quarterback Kurt Warner was named most valuable player in the National Football League. How, then, could Rams running back Marshall Faulk be recognized as NFL offensive player of the year?

If it sounds like a contradiction, Faulk says it's not.

"MVP is for value to the team; offensive player of the year is for productivity," said Faulk, whose teammates voted him Rams MVP. "Could we have won as many games without me? Maybe. Without Kurt? I don't know."

Though Faulk became just the second NFL player to gain more than 1,000 yards receiving and more than 1,000 rushing in the same season — San Francisco's Roger Craig did it in 1985 — Faulk said there might have been ways to get past his own absence.

But Rams coach Dick Vermeil is among those who believe Faulk's presence changes the essence of the team. "He turns the boost up on our engine beyond league rules," said Vermeil, an auto racing enthusiast.

Yet Faulk said his motor could have sputtered if not for the splendid efforts all around him.

"I mean, there's five guys up front who work very hard to get me yardage," Faulk said of his offensive line. "They bust their butts, but they never get the (accolades). They've kept people off of me, they've blocked downfield, they've blocked at the point of attack."

Faulk also gushes about the blocking of fullback Robert Holcombe and the Rams receivers. And then there was Warner. His greatest trait is poise, Faulk said.

The Rams led the NFL in scoring with 526 points. Regardless of how the awards played out or his appreciation for his teammates, Faulk's contributions were substantial: He rushed 253 times for 1,381 yards and seven touchdowns and had 87 receptions for 1,048 yards and five TDs. His combined yardage, 2,429, is an NFL record.

Faulk did it with flabbergasting moves and surprising power for a man only 5 feet 10, 210 pounds. But it's the eyes on his face that might best reflect the Marshall arts.

"He runs with his eyes probably as well as any back in pro football, probably in the history of pro football," Rams vice president of player personnel Charley Armey said. "His legs allow him to do what his instincts and eyes tell him to do."

Teammates point to his poise and awareness. His consciousness can be seen in his fluid running style, which is predicated on more than just his 4.3-second speed in the 40-yard dash.

"He has unbelievable, impeccable timing," defensive tackle D'Marco Farr said. "Most of the time, he's waiting for you to make a mistake, but on the flip side of that, if you wait for him to make a move he's already by you."

Ask most observers about what makes Faulk special, and "instinct" always comes up. But that doesn't give Faulk enough credit. It is an acquired talent. No one, for instance, watches more film of opponents than Faulk does.

"He gives himself an edge because he prepares himself like no other individual I've seen," said running backs coach Wilbert Montgomery, who usually arrives at work Monday morning to find Faulk waiting in his office already having studied film. "He takes it to the extreme."

EVERYONE ELSE BEGINS TO BELIEVE

—◇—

By Jim Thomas

S tage fright? Uh-uh.

"Well, so much for not having any playoff experience," coach Dick Vermeil said sarcastically.

Soft schedule? Doesn't matter.

Perhaps the sign, hoisted by one of the 66,194 zanies in the Trans World Dome, said it best: "We STILL haven't played anybody."

Minnesota coach Dennis Green said his Vikings played 60 minutes of football. He needs to get his watch fixed.

Yes, the Vikings hung in for a half. In fact, the visitors from the North led 17-14 at intermission. But then, Tony Horne took the opening kickoff of the second half 95 yards for a touchdown. And before long, a dance festival broke out. Featuring, of course, the Bob & Weave.

Kurt Warner's fifth touchdown pass of the game gave St. Louis a 49-17 lead midway through the fourth quarter. The Vikings scored three late touchdowns to make the final score 49-37 — St. Louis — but they were merely cosmetic points, so much rouge to hide the warts in the Minnesota pass defense.

The Rams' scorched-earth offense took no prisoners in the NFC semifinal playoff game. Warner threw five TD passes — to five different receivers.

The Rams clobbered the Vikings with their talent and with the playbook of offensive coordinator Mike Martz. The Rams set 25 team and individual playoff records.

Things got so absurd that in one second-half sequence, converted defensive end Jeff Robinson and No. 3 offensive tackle Ryan Tucker caught TD passes.

All of which made the first home playoff game in St. Louis football history well worth the wait.

"This win is so big for the team, so big for the city, and so big for the organization," said cornerback Todd Lyght. "We're really catapulting ourselves in the right direction, and I think we're going to be a tough team for a couple years."

Torry Holt led more than 66,000 fans at the Trans World Dome in the latest version of Dance Fever after Isaac Bruce's first-quarter TD catch.

Isaac Bruce (right) and Torry Holt began issuing stage directions for the postseason reprise of the Bob & Weave after Bruce's 77-yard touchdown pass on the Rams' first play from scrimmage.

Tony Horne threw the first haymaker of the second half, a 95-yard return on the opening kickoff that gave the Rams a 21-17 lead and sent them off on their 35-point run.

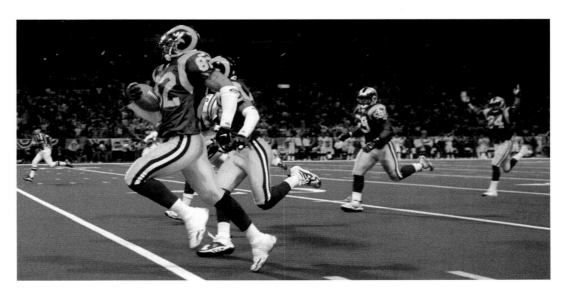

Kurt Warner & Co. delivered a blow that sent the NFC's established order topsy-turvy when they erupted for a 35-point blitz in less than 22 minutes of the divisional playoff at the Trans World Dome.

Tim Hill of Ballwin, Mo., got prepared — with a little help from his 'friends' — to put the Ram-rush on the Vikings.

ROAD TO THE SUPER BOWL

NFC divisional playoff game

Rams 49
Vikings 37

Down go the Vikings in the Rams' 2nd-half

KNOCKOUT

When do the Rams play next?

They play host to the **Tampa Bay Buccaneers** at 2:15 p.m. Sunday (KTVI, Channel 2) with a Super Bowl berth on the line. The Rams offense, ranked No. 1 in the NFL's regular season, will square off against the third-ranked Bucs defense, led by Warren Sapp. The opening Las Vegas odds favor the Rams by 14 points.

How to buy tickets

A total of 2,500 tickets to the NFC Championship Game will **go on sale at 11 a.m. today** through Ticketmaster and the Trans World Dome box office. Ticketmaster will not offer sales via the Internet.

In the AFC

Eddie George carried the **Tennessee Titans** into the AFC Championship Game.

Warner's record day pushes Rams to NFC title game

By Jim Thomas
Of the Post-Dispatch

KEY TO THE GAME

The Rams broke the game open in the third quarter, their best quarter of the season: Tony Horne ran the second-half kickoff back for a touchdown, the Rams offense scored two touchdowns and the defense held the Vikings to negative yardage.

Billy Jenkins planted Jeff George on a safety blitz. The Rams' pressure, which included some well-designed blitzes, got to George four times for 35 yards in losses.

	1ST	2ND	3RD	4TH	TOTAL
VIKINGS	3	14	0	20	37
RAMS	14	0	21	14	49

SCORING SUMMARY

QTR	TEAM	PLAY		TIME
1st	**VIKINGS**	FG	Anderson 31 yds.	9:23
1st	**RAMS**	TD	Bruce 77 yd. pass from Warner (Wilkins kick)	9:02
1st	**RAMS**	TD	Faulk 41 yd. pass from Warner (Wilkins kick)	4:19
2nd	**VIKINGS**	TD	Carter 22 yd. pass from George (Anderson kick)	9:53
2nd	**VIKINGS**	TD	Hoard 4 yd. run (Anderson kick)	2:40
3rd	**RAMS**	TD	Horne 95 yd. kickoff return (Wilkins kick)	14:42
3rd	**RAMS**	TD	Faulk 1 yd. run (Wilkins kick)	8:28
3rd	**RAMS**	TD	Robinson 13 yd. pass from Warner (Wilkins kick)	:22
4th	**RAMS**	TD	Tucker 1 yd. pass from Warner (Wilkins kick)	13:36
4th	**RAMS**	TD	Williams 2 yd. pass from Warner (Wilkins kick)	8:13
4th	**VIKINGS**	TD	Reed 4 yd. pass from George (2 pt. conversion: Hoard run)	4:56
4th	**VIKINGS**	TD	Moss 44 yd. pass from George (2 pt. failed)	3:48
4th	**VIKINGS**	TD	Moss 2 yd. pass from George (2 pt. failed)	:31

OFFENSE

RAMS

PASSING	ATT	COMP	YDS	INT	TD
Kurt Warner	33	27	391	1	5

RECEIVING	CATCHES	YDS	TD
Torry Holt	6	65	
Marshall Faulk	5	80	1
Az-Zahir Hakim	5	49	
Isaac Bruce	4	133	1
Roland Williams	2	20	1
Jeff Robinson	1	13	1
Robert Holcombe	1	12	
Ricky Proehl	1	10	
Ernie Conwell	1	8	
Ryan Tucker	1	1	1

RUSHING	RUSHES	YDS	TD
Marshall Faulk	11	21	1
Az-Zahir Hakim	1	4	
Kurt Warner	3	3	
Robert Holcombe	1	2	
Amp Lee	1	1	

VIKINGS

PASSING	ATT	COMP	YDS	INT	TD
Jeff George	50	29	424	1	4

RECEIVING	CATCHES	YDS	TD
Randy Moss	9	188	2
Cris Carter	7	106	1
Robert Smith	7	32	
Jake Reed	5	85	1
Andrew Glover	1	12	

RUSHING	RUSHES	YDS	TD
Robert Smith	20	64	
Leroy Hoard	7	24	1
Jeff George	2	-1	

Jeff George, the Vikings quarterback, saw the game slip away during a pivotal stretch of the second half. In the Vikes' first four possessions, he was just two of eight passing for minus 9 yards. He also lost a fumble and had a delay-of-game penalty.

143

66 *It's beginning to look like the St. Louis Rams haven't played anybody* 99
because they are turning everybody into nobody.

Don Pierson, Chicago Tribune

Tom Wilkens (left) and brother Steve of Waterloo, Ill., get in character as the Ram Bandwagon rolls over the Vikings for another touchdown.

Kurt Warner, having torched the Vikings for 391 yards passing, cooled down as he waited to be interviewed afterward.

FINAL TAKE

By Bernie Miklasz

What Dick Vermeil has done is build the perfect beast.

His football team has an old-school toughness, just like the brawny squad of Rocky Balboas he had in Philadelphia. But he has taken those old-fashioned 1970s values and has decorated them with a modern offense that's something beautiful, something to behold.

Dick Vermeil's St. Louis Rams can knock you down, bloody your mouth and then dissect you with surgical, almost scientific precision. How can something so pretty inflict so many bruises? If you happen to push these Rams back, they'll come right back at you with beefy knuckles and hard heads.

Blue collars, gold glitter. Rams colors.

The Rams can beat you with finesse; they can beat you in the clinches. They dazzle and confuse you with sorcery; they wear you down with strength and stamina. It's Air Coryell on andro. The X's and O's are so sensational as to be cruel, with offensive mastermind Mike Martz sending plays down from the booth like some deranged Dr. Frankenstein.

You have Vermeil's Philadelphia and Martz's freedom. You have Vermeil's golden oldies and Martz's hip hop. When this Best of the '70s, Best of the '90s hybrid takes to the magic carpet, the speed thrills and it kills.

At the Transformation Dome, the Minnesota Vikings were shown some rare mercy. The Rams committed enough mistakes to give the Vikings a slight opening, a chance to pilfer this NFC playoff game. The sneaky Vikes led 17-14 at the half, but then the Rams fine-tuned the machine.

By the time the roar of the engine and the roar of the crowd subsided, the Vikings were down 49-17 and reduced to speed bumps. The Rams raced and glided right over them.

Georgia Frontiere was able to herald the Rise of the Ram after her team already had served notice by pasting the Vikings and advancing to the NFC Championship Game.

PROEHL'S CATCH IS SIMPLY SUPER

———— ◇ ————

BY JIM THOMAS

From Baltimore to Minnesota, the Rams scored 73 touchdowns this season. Everyone from Isaac Bruce to James Hodgins to Ryan Tucker reached the end zone. They all had the chance to Bob & Weave.

Ricky Proehl could only watch — until Jan. 23, that is. That's when Proehl made the play of his life, a touchdown catch unlike any seen previously in St. Louis football history.

His 30-yard TD reception from Kurt Warner gave the Rams an 11-6 victory over Tampa Bay in the NFC Championship Game. As a result, the Rams are going to the Super Bowl in Atlanta.

Do not adjust your newspaper. It's true. The previously sadsack St. Louis Rams are "taking Georgia to Georgia" to play Tennessee in the Super Bowl.

"We won four games last year," safety Keith Lyle said. "Trent Green gets hurt. I said, 'Oh man, not this.' If a psychic would have told me we were going to the Super Bowl in Atlanta, I would have asked for my money back."

No refund will be necessary, thanks to Proehl, who made the clutchest of clutch catches on third and 4 from the Tampa Bay 30 with 4 minutes 44 seconds to play.

During a timeout before the play, Warner reminded Proehl: If the safety blitzes, run a fade — or deep — route. If the Bucs were in a normal defense, and didn't blitz, Proehl was supposed to run an 18-yard — or sideline — route.

The Bucs blitzed the free safety. So Proehl went deep down the left sideline and outfought Buccaneers nickel back Brian Kelly for the ball in the end zone.

"I've played for 10 years, and the best I've been is 8-8. Never seen the playoffs," Proehl said. "This is what I've dreamed about for years."

Proehl finally got to Bob & Weave. It was not a thing of beauty.

"You know what? I don't care," said Proehl, 31. "We're going to Atlanta."

Ricky Proehl, with six catches for 100 yards, kept the Rams pointed in the right direction on a day in which first downs were hard to come by.

Grant Wistrom, who had four solo tackles, including a key sack, signaled a safety after a high snap eluded quarterback Shaun King and King batted the ball out of the end zone in the second quarter.

Billy Jenkins (right) put the heat on Jacquez Green, who couldn't haul in this third-quarter pass from Shaun King.

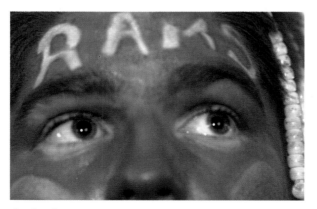

St. Louisans put on an intense game face for the first pro football title game in the city's history.

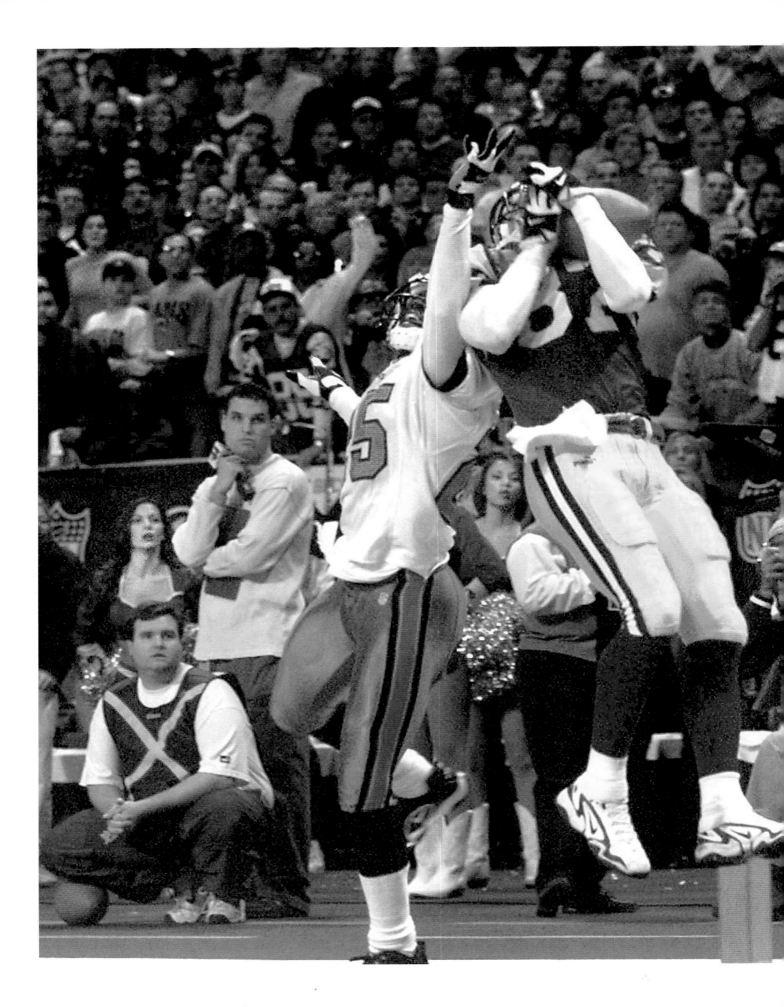

Ricky Proehl came up with his first touchdown catch of the season when the Rams desperately needed it, yanking the NFC title away from cornerback Brian Kelly and the Bucs. "They made a great play, and they capitalized on it," Kelly said.

Tom Nutten (61) and Isaac Bruce gave Ricky
Proehl a lift in the end zone after helping the
Rams rise above a Tampa Bay defense that
held them to 309 total yards from scrimmage.

Dick Vermeil tried to use every ounce of body language he could as the Rams stopped Tampa Bay's final drive.

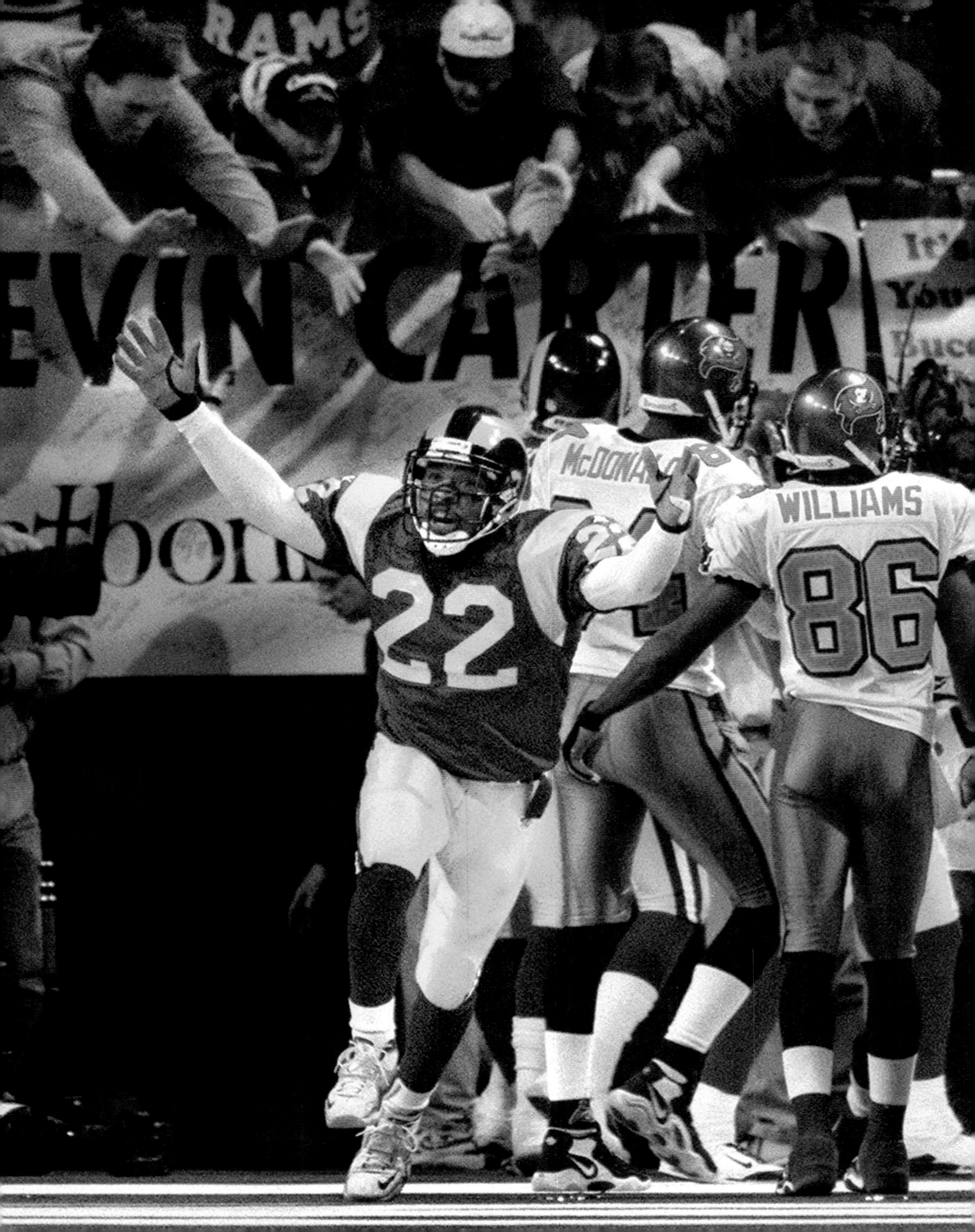
RAMS
EVIN CARTER
22
WILLIAMS
86

Billy Jenkins began his sprint for Atlanta after the Bucs' last-gasp, fourth-down fling had been batted down in the end zone in the final minute.

After about three decades of NFL frustration, more than 66,000 fans at the Trans World Dome were emphatic that one is NOT the loneliest number.

	1ST	2ND	3RD	4TH	TOTAL
BUCS	3	0	3	0	6
RAMS	3	2	0	6	11

SCORING SUMMARY

QTR	TEAM	PLAY	TIME
1st	**BUCS**	FG Gramatica 25 yds.	12:22
1st	**RAMS**	FG Wilkins 24 yds.	4:17
2nd	**RAMS**	SFT King knocked ball out of end zone	14:55
3rd	**BUCS**	FG Gramatica 23 yds.	10:28
4th	**RAMS**	TD Proehl 30 yd. pass from Warner (2 pt. failed)	4:44

OFFENSE

BUCCANEERS

PASSING	ATT	COMP	YDS	INT	TD
Shaun King	29	13	163	2	0

RECEIVING	CATCHES	YDS	TD
Jacquez Green	4	59	
Warrick Dunn	4	37	
Karl Williams	2	28	
Bert Emanuel	1	22	
Mike Alstott	1	9	
David Moore	1	8	

RUSHING	RUSHES	YDS	TD
Mike Alstott	12	39	
Warrick Dunn	9	35	
Shaun King	2	3	

RAMS

PASSING	ATT	COMP	YDS	INT	TD
Kurt Warner	43	26	258	3	1

RECEIVING	CATCHES	YDS	TD
Torry Holt	7	68	
Ricky Proehl	6	100	1
Isaac Bruce	3	22	
Marshall Faulk	3	5	
Az-Zahir Hakim	2	27	
Robert Holcombe	2	5	
Roland Williams	1	22	
Jeff Robinson	1	11	
Ernie Conwell	1	–2	

RUSHING	RUSHES	YDS	TD
Marshall Faulk	17	44	
Az-Zahir Hakim	1	6	
Robert Holcombe	1	2	
Kurt Warner	2	–1	

KEY TO THE GAME

Tampa Bay had the ball and a 6-5 lead midway through the fourth quarter, but rookie Dre' Bly came up with a crucial interception and returned the ball to the Bucs 47. Six plays later, Kurt Warner hit Ricky Proehl with a 30-yard touchdown pass that put the Rams in the Super Bowl.

Dexter McCleon exulted in the closing seconds. McCleon was part of a Rams secondary that held Tampa Bay to just 163 yards passing.

155

Kurt Warner, with another chapter in his storybook season written, took a victory lap around the Trans World Dome with game ball in hand. In the background is the George Halas Trophy, just over the right shoulder of the man who helped the Rams seize it.

Champions at last, **Ricky Proehl** (center) and his Rams teammates hoisted the George Halas Trophy that goes to the winner of the NFC. "I've played for 10 years, and the best I've been is 8-8. Never seen the playoffs. This is what I've dreamed about for years," Proehl said.

FINAL TAKE

BY BERNIE MIKLASZ

The Rams would have to get to the Super Bowl the hard way. They would have to go counting bruises and welts instead of yards and touchdowns. They would have to wrestle the alligators from Tampa, and the beast chewed them up for most of the day.

The cute offense was put in storage as the two teams engaged in a medieval scrum. This football game was like some of those battlefield scenes from the film Braveheart. Rams wide receiver Torry Holt got popped in the ribs and coughed up blood, and returned to play. Wide receiver Az-Zahir Hakim missed four series with dehydration. Bodies were tumbling, cracking. It became an ordeal to navigate every yard.

And in the end, the Rams were just a little stronger, tougher and determined. The Rams connected with the last punch, and the Bucs fell.

The Rams' defense nev-er rested. It's one of the roughest, meanest units in the league. The defense saved the season. By not surrendering anything more than two field goals, the defense held the fort until the offense made a late rescue.

And this team is more than just speed and a playbook. These guys can hit. They can play tackle football. The Rams beat the Bucs at their own game. The Rams may be a pretty team, but they're capable of winning ugly.

The Rams gave themselves, and this city, one of the greatest moments in St. Louis sports history. And it wasn't easy. It required lots of blood and sweat. And only then could the teardrops fall.

"Standing out there, with all of those guys that you've worked with, and bled with, and cried with," D'Marco Farr said. "It was the most emotion I've ever felt. I wish everybody could experience this."

We did.

Georgia Frontiere joined thousands of St. Louisans who were looking up to Kurt Warner after he made another clutch throw in the game's last five minutes.

157

RAMS 23 TITANS 16 SuperBowl

"HERE WE ARE, CHAMPS"

—————— ◇ ——————

BY JIM THOMAS

How about it, St. Louis? Super Bowl champions. Doesn't that have a nice ring to it?

The Rams put the Tennessee Titans on ice in a memorable Super Bowl XXXIV, but only on the final play of the game. Out of timeouts with six seconds to play and the ball on the Rams 10-yard line, Titans quarterback Steve McNair took one last shot at the end zone and overtime, throwing to Kevin Dyson at the 5. Dyson made a hard cut toward the end zone . . . then along came Jones.

Outside linebacker Mike Jones, the pride of the University of Missouri, wrapped up Dyson with a textbook tackle at the 1 as time expired.

The Rams were Super Bowl champions with a white-knuckle, 23-16 victory over Tennessee. They took Georgia to Georgia, and Georgia took the Lombardi Trophy back to the Gateway to the West.

"It proves that we did the right thing in going to St. Louis," owner Georgia Frontiere said defiantly as she accepted the Lombardi Trophy from NFL Commissioner Paul Tagliabue, who tried to block the club's move to St. Louis from Southern California in 1995. "This trophy belongs to our coach, our team and our fans in St. Louis."

The Rams did it with a Super Bowl-record 414 yards passing by Super Bowl most valuable player Kurt Warner. They did it after squandering a 16-0 lead in the final $1\frac{1}{2}$ quarters.

In the end, it was wide receiver Isaac Bruce who provided the margin of victory, on a shot heard 'round the world — a 73-yard touchdown pass from Warner with 1:54 to play.

Then, the Rams had to hold on. And they did, just barely.

"Here we are, champs," cornerback Todd Lyght said. "We brought the championship back to the city of St. Louis, and they deserve it."

Kurt Warner and Isaac Bruce shared a championship embrace. Warner, who once had stocked groceries at an Iowa supermarket, had truly earned the right to be called top-shelf: NFL MVP, Super Bowl MVP and a Super Bowl-record 414 passing yards.

Roland Williams did a screen test of the Bob & Weave for MTV on media day. Williams, a Rams tight end, didn't get much camera time on Super Sunday (one catch for 9 yards), but with 414 yards in catches and two touchdowns, the St. Louis air game got ample air time.

The days leading up to the Super Bowl gave Rams fans a chance to reflect their spirit to the world. **Kathy McCandless** of St. Louis waited for her hair to dry at a local beauty salon while the city's universal message projected out from the window behind her.

Despite Tennessee's best efforts to gum up the works, dentist **Dan Walde** of Washington, Mo., had a world title to celebrate with his fellow Rams fans.

Todd Lyght burst through in the third quarter to block Al Del Greco's 47-yard field-goal attempt. The play set up the Rams for a 68-yard touchdown drive that gave them a 16-0 lead.

A 28-PAGE SUPER BOWL SECTION BEGINS ON D1

ST. LOUIS POST-DISPATCH

MONDAY, JANUARY 31, 2000

SUPER HEROES

Kurt Warner leads the way.

Isaac Bruce makes the play.

Billy Jenkins (right) wrestled Titans tight end Frank Wycheck to the ground after a short gain in the third quarter.

Isaac Bruce adjusted to the flight of the ball and grabbed Kurt Warner's pass in front of Denard Walker, before racing off with the winning 73-yard TD catch with 1:54 remaining.

	1ST	2ND	3RD	4TH	TOTAL
RAMS	3	6	7	7	23
TITANS	0	0	6	10	16

SCORING SUMMARY

QTR	TEAM	PLAY	TIME
1st	**RAMS**	FG Wilkins 27 yds.	3:00
2nd	**RAMS**	FG Wilkins 29 yds.	4:16
2nd	**RAMS**	FG Wilkins 28 yds.	:15
3rd	**RAMS**	TD Holt 9 yd. pass from Warner (Wilkins kick)...........	7:20
3rd	**TITANS**	TD George 1 yd. run (2 pt. pass failed)	:14
4th	**TITANS**	TD George 2 yd. run (Del Greco kick)........................	7:21
4th	**TITANS**	FG Del Greco 43 yds.	2:12
4th	**RAMS**	TD Bruce 73 yd. pass from Warner (Wilkins kick)	1:54

KEY TO THE GAME

With the ball on the Rams 10 and six seconds left, Titans quarterback Steve McNair hit Kevin Dyson on a slant-in pass at the 5-yard line for what seemed like the inside track to the end zone. But linebacker Mike Jones, in one-on-one coverage, hauled down Dyson at the 1 as time ran out to preserve St. Louis' first NFL title.

OFFENSE

RAMS

PASSING	ATT	COMP	YDS	INT	TD
Kurt Warner	45	24	414	0	2

RECEIVING	CATCHES	YDS	TD
Isaac Bruce	6	162	1
Torry Holt	7	109	1
Marshall Faulk	5	90	
Az-Zahir Hakim	1	17	
Ricky Proehl	1	11	
Roland Williams	1	9	
Robert Holcombe	1	1	
Fred Miller	1	–1	

RUSHING	RUSHES	YDS	TD
Marshall Faulk	10	17	
Robert Holcombe	1	11	
Kurt Warner	1	1	
Mike Horan	1	0	

TITANS

PASSING	ATT	COMP	YDS	INT	TD
Steve McNair	36	22	214	0	0

RECEIVING	CATCHES	YDS	TD
Jackie Harris	7	64	
Kevin Dyson	4	41	
Frank Wycheck	5	35	
Eddie George	2	35	
Isaac Byrd	2	21	
Derrick Mason	2	18	

RUSHING	RUSHES	YDS	TD
Eddie George	28	95	2
Steve McNair	8	64	

Todd Lyght (41) helped the Rams come to grips with the Titans offense early. The Rams held Tennessee to just 89 yards of total offense in the opening half.

Jay Williams (96) and Kevin Carter scrambled frantically after quarterback Steve McNair on the Titans' last-ditch drive. McNair bedeviled the Rams with 278 yards of total offense.

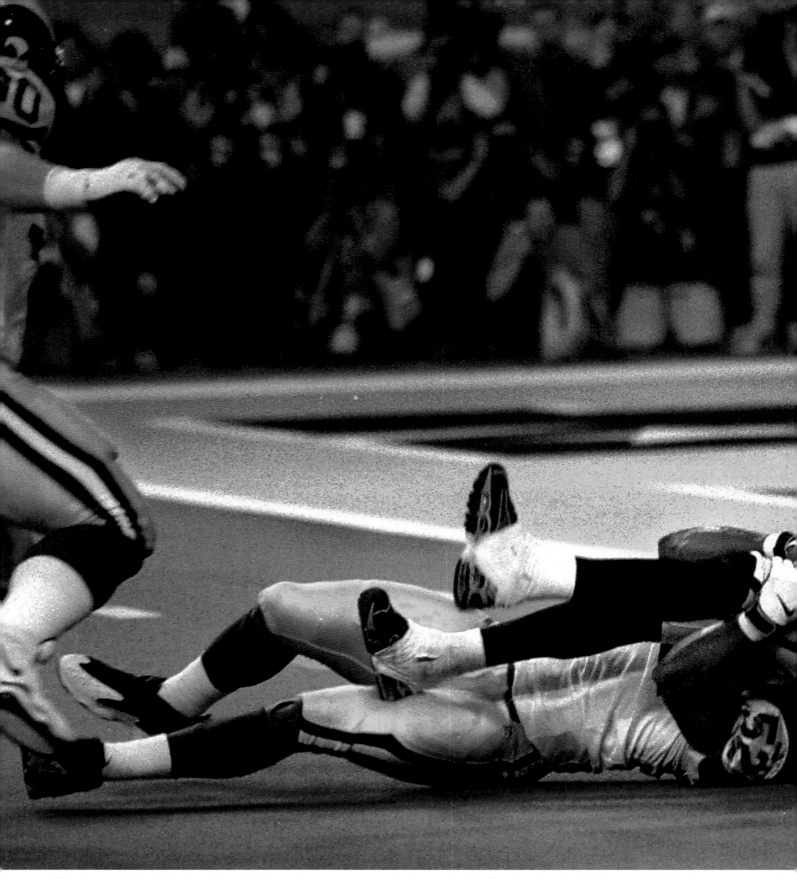

Mike Jones, dubbed "Hands of Stone" by his teasing teammates, made the catch of his life when he pulled in Tennessee's Kevin Dyson a yard from the goal line as time ran out to give the Rams the world title. "I know Tennessee thought they were a team of destiny," Jones said. "We thought it was our destiny to win this game."

Isaac Bruce hauled in six receptions for 162 yards, but the catch of the night was the Lombardi Trophy, which signified a season of prayers answered for Rev. Ike and his teammates.

Dick Vermeil left the field with his wife Carol as a world champion, 19 years after absorbing Super Bowl frustration as coach of the Philadelphia Eagles.

Georgia Frontiere and Dick Vermeil completed the Rams' 19-game trophy dash with the ultimate prize. "I'd rather win 32-0 to tell ya the truth," Vermeil said. "But in terms of the American football fan, it had to be great to watch."

" I always believed in myself. I had a whole bunch of people who believed in me . . . We're world champions! How 'bout them Rams!"

Kurt Warner, at the Lombardi Trophy presentation

After the Rams had finished off another Warner Bros. production in front of a worldwide audience, the fans celebrated at Planet Hollywood on Laclede's Landing in St. Louis.

Eddie George, the shreds of victory pouring down around him, tried to come to grips with the heartbreaking defeat. George finished with 95 yards on 28 carries. "They're great warriors," Rams linebacker Mike Jones said of the Titans.

SuperBowl

RAMS	23
TITANS	16

FINAL TAKE

BY BERNIE MIKLASZ

One tackle made Mike Jones a hero. One tackle made the world spin, made hearts stop and took everyone's breath away. One tackle turned the Rams into world champions.

One tackle started a flow of champagne in St. Louis and the flow of tears in Tennessee. One tackle forced NFL Commissioner Paul Tagliabue to present the Lombardi Trophy to Rams owner Georgia Frontiere with millions of people watching. One tackle gave Georgia the sweetest revenge against the league that tried to stop her from moving to St. Louis.

One tackle decided the greatest Super Bowl ever played.

It was one tackle, on the last play of the game, made a yard from the St. Louis end zone. It gave us memories that will last a lifetime. It sends Mike Jones, the Rams outside linebacker, right into that special place where the legends live forever. He's up there now with Bob Gibson striking out all those Tigers, Mark McGwire hitting Nos. 62 and 70, Willie McGee climbing the walls and hitting home runs in the 1982 World Series.

We will be talking about it for the rest of our lives, and our kids will tell their kids, and it will be passed on through the generations.

We will talk about how Tennessee, trailing 23-16, marched down the field. Suddenly, the Titans were at the 10-yard line with six seconds left. We will talk about how Titans quarterback Steve McNair threw a pass to wide receiver Kevin Dyson, who caught the ball inside the 5-yard line and tried to curl into the end zone.

Jones flew across the carpet to make the rescue.

"That, right there, was the greatest tackle made in Super Bowl history," Rams safety Keith Lyle said. "The rest of our lives, we'll see that shown a million times on TV, and we'll replay it over and over again in our minds."

The Lombardi Trophy was finally in the clutches of the Rams after a dramatic 23-16 victory.

Vermeilretires **Vermeilretires** Vermeilretires

FINAL TAKE

BY BERNIE MIKLASZ

It was the perfect, happy ending. Dick Vermeil deserved to go out as a champion. He had no more mountains to climb, personal or professional.

He conquered himself, controlling the obsessive, consuming behavior that drove him out of coaching in 1983.

After losing 23 of 32 games in his first two seasons in St. Louis, he adapted to his players and the league and earned the affection and the respect of his team.

After nearly being fired a year earlier, Vermeil won over his critics. He built just what he had in the glory days in Philadelphia — a tough, caring family circle — and combined it with a prolific offense. It was the ideal blend of old-school football and new-age football.

The players loved him. The assistants loved him. The fans loved him. The owners loved him. And then, he won the greatest Super Bowl ever played.

This was probably the finest one-year coaching job in NFL history. Vermeil took a sorry, no-account 4-12 team and made it a champion.

He made St. Louis, the place that the NFL had kicked around for so long, the league's new title town.

And he did all this with class. We may see a better football coach in St. Louis, but we'll never be so fortunate to have a better person coaching the Rams. The squad that won the Super Bowl was a wonderful reflection of his personality.

Now, more than 40 years after entering this profession, Vermeil has made his second and final retirement. And this one is so much sweeter. When he retired from the Eagles, Vermeil left without a Super Bowl ring. He left without finding inner peace. Restless, he returned to search for those things. And now, he has them. He's a champion. He's happy.

And he leaves after making St. Louis a champion, too.

Thanks, DV.

Wins sometimes were secondary on **Dick Vermeil's** journey. "The high of coaching for me is the relationship with the players," he said while choking back emotions during his retirement announcement.

NFL MOST VALUABLE PLAYER	NFL OFFENSIVE PLAYER OF THE YEAR	NFL COACH OF THE YEAR
Kurt Warner	**Marshall Faulk**	**Dick Vermeil**

PRO BOWL STARTERS

Kurt Warner, quarterback	Isaac Bruce, wide receiver	Kevin Carter, defensive end
Marshall Faulk, running back	Orlando Pace, offensive tackle	Todd Lyght, cornerback

REGULAR-SEASON STATISTICAL LEADERS AND ROSTER

DEFENSE

INTERCEPTIONS

	No.	Yds.	Avg.	Lg.	TD
Lyght	6	112	18.7	57t	1
M. Jones	4	96	24.0	44t	2
McCleon	4	17	4.3	14	0
Bly	3	53	17.7	53t	1
Wistrom	2	131	65.5	91t	2
Allen	2	76	38.0	40	0
Bush	2	45	22.5	45t	1
Jenkins	2	16	8.0	14	0
Lyle	2	10	5.0	10	0
Rams	29	567	19.6	91t	7
Opp.	15	266	17.7	60	2

SACKS

Carter	17.0
Farr	8.5
Wistrom	6.5
Zgonina	4.5
J. Williams	4.0
Clemons	3.0
Fletcher	3.0
Agnew	2.5
Lyght	2.5
McCleon	1.5
Jenkins	1.0
M. Jones	1.0
Lyle	1.0
Rams	57.0
Opp.	33.0

TACKLES

	No.	Solo	Ast.
Fletcher	138	80	58
Jenkins	116	84	32
M. Jones	94	58	36
Collins	74	41	33
Lyght	65	50	15
Wistrom	60	37	23
Agnew	56	30	26
McCleon	54	45	9
Bush	50	38	12
Farr	48	32	16

SPECIAL TEAMS

PUNTING

	No.	Yds.	Avg.	Inside 20	Lg.
Horan	26	1048	40.3	7	57
Tuten	32	1359	42.5	9	70
Wilkins	2	57	28.5	1	34
Rams	60	2464	41.1	17	70
Opp.	86	3674	42.7	26	65

PUNT RETURNS

	No.	FC	Yds.	Avg.	Lg.	TD
Hakim	44	22	461	10.5	84t	1
Horne	5	0	22	4.4	9	0
Holt	3	2	15	5.0	11	0
Rams	52	24	498	9.6	84t	1
Opp.	23	7	155	6.7	20	0

KICKOFF RETURNS

	No.	Yds.	Avg.	Lg.	TD
Horne	30	892	29.7	101t	2
Carpenter	16	406	25.4	43	0
Rams	54	1354	25.1	101t	2
Opp.	85	2115	24.9	69	0

FIELD GOALS

	1-19	20-29	30-39	40-49	50+
Wilkins	1-1	5-5	6-7	7-11	1-4
Opp.	1-1	8-9	2-4	8-9	1-3

OFFENSE

PASSING

	Att.	Cmp.	Pct.	Yds.	TD	Int.	Lg.
Warner	499	325	65.1	4353	41	13	75t
Germaine	16	9	56.3	136	1	2	63t
Justin	14	9	64.3	91	0	0	27
Rams	530	343	64.7	4580	42	15	75t
Opp.	596	319	53.5	3867	19	29	71t

Rating: Warner 109.2   Rams 106.6

RECEIVING

	Att.	Yds.	Avg.	Lg.	TD
Faulk	87	1048	12.0	57t	5
Bruce	77	1165	15.1	60	12
Holt	52	788	15.2	63t	6
Hakim	36	677	18.8	75t	8
Proehl	33	349	10.6	30	0
R. Williams	25	226	9.0	24	6
Holcombe	14	163	11.6	30	1
Robinson	6	76	12.7	30	2
Hodgins	6	35	5.8	10	0
Lee	3	22	7.3	15t	1
Rams	343	4580	13.4	75t	42
Opp.	319	3867	12.1	71t	19

RUSHING

	Att.	Yds.	Avg.	Lg.	TD
Faulk	253	1381	5.5	58	7
Holcombe	78	294	3.8	34	4
Watson	47	179	3.8	21	0
Warner	23	92	4.0	22	1
Hakim	4	44	11.0	31	0
Bruce	5	32	6.4	11	0
Holt	3	25	8.3	14	0
Hodgins	7	10	1.4	3	1
Lee	3	3	1.0	4	0
Rams	431	2059	4.8	58	13
Opp.	338	1189	3.5	40	4

TEAM

	Rams	Opp.
Total first downs	335	263
3rd down: made/att	91/194	77/228
3rd down pct.	46.9	33.8
Time of possession avg.	31:50	28:10
Total net yards	6412	4698
Avg. per game	400.8	293.6
Net yards rushing	2059	1189
Avg. per game	128.7	74.3
Net yards passing	4353	3509
Avg. per game	272.1	219.3
Sacked/yards lost	33/227	57/358
Penalties/yards	113/889	114/1007
Touchdowns	66	26
Rushing	13	4
Passing	42	19
Returns	11	3

#	NAME	POS.	HT.	WT.	YR.	COLLEGE
2	Mike Horan	P	5-11	192	17	Long Beach St.
9	Joe Germaine	QB	6-0	203	R	Ohio State
11	Rick Tuten	P	6-2	221	11	Florida St.
13	Kurt Warner	QB	6-2	220	2	Northern Iowa
14	Jeff Wilkins	K	6-2	205	6	Youngstown St.
16	Paul Justin	QB	6-4	211	5	Arizona State
20	Taje Allen	DB	5-10	185	3	Texas
21	Dexter McCleon	RC	5-10	195	3	Clemson
22	Billy Jenkins	SS	5-10	205	3	Howard
23	Devin Bush	SS	6-0	210	5	Florida State
24	Ron Carpenter	S	6-1	188	3	Miami (Ohio)
25	Robert Holcombe	FB	5-11	220	2	Illinois
28	Marshall Faulk	RB	5-10	211	6	San Diego St.
31	Amp Lee	RB	5-11	200	8	Florida State
32	Dre' Bly	DB	5-9	185	R	North Carolina
35	Keith Lyle	FS	6-2	210	6	Virginia
36	Justin Watson	RB	6-0	225	1	San Diego St.
38	Rich Coady	FS	6-0	203	R	Texas A&M
41	Todd Lyght	LC	6-0	190	9	Notre Dame
42	James Hodgins	FB	5-11	230	R	San Jose State
45	Jeff Robinson	TE	6-4	275	7	Idaho
50	Ryan Tucker	C	6-5	305	3	Texas Christian
51	Lorenzo Styles	MLB	6-1	245	5	Ohio State
52	Mike Jones	LLB	6-1	240	9	Missouri
54	Todd Collins	RLB	6-2	248	7	Carson-Newman
56	Charlie Clemons	MLB	6-2	255	3	Georgia
57	Leonard Little	LB	6-3	237	2	Tennessee
58	Mike Morton	OLB	6-4	235	5	North Carolina
59	London Fletcher	MLB	5-10	241	2	John Carroll
60	Mike Gruttadauria	C	6-3	297	4	Central Florida
61	Tom Nutten	LG	6-5	300	3	W. Michigan
62	Adam Timmerman	RG	6-4	300	5	S. Dakota St.
64	Andy McCollum	C	6-4	295	6	Toledo
71	Cameron Spikes	G	6-2	310	R	Texas A&M
73	Fred Miller	RT	6-7	315	4	Baylor
75	D'Marco Farr	DT	6-1	280	6	Washington
76	Orlando Pace	LT	6-7	320	3	Ohio State
77	Matt Willig	OT	6-7	315	7	USC
80	Isaac Bruce	WR	6-0	188	6	Memphis
81	Az-Zahir Hakim	WR	5-10	179	2	San Diego St.
82	Tony Horne	WR	5-9	173	2	Clemson
83	Chris Thomas	WR	6-2	190	4	Cal-Poly SLO
84	Ernie Conwell	TE	6-1	265	4	Washington
86	Roland Williams	TE	6-5	269	2	Syracuse
87	Ricky Proehl	WR	6-0	190	10	Wake Forest
88	Torry Holt	WR	6-0	190	R	N.C. State
90	Jeff Zgonina	DT	6-2	300	7	Purdue
91	Troy Pelshak	RLB	6-2	242	R	N.C. A&T
92	Lionel Barnes	DE	6-4	265	R	La.-Monroe
93	Kevin Carter	DE	6-5	280	5	Florida
95	N. Hobgood-Chittick	DT	6-3	290	2	North Carolina
96	Jay Williams	DE	6-3	280	4	Wake Forest
98	Grant Wistrom	DE	6-4	267	2	Nebraska
99	Ray Agnew	DT	6-3	285	10	N.C. State